The Zen
Master's
Dance

# The Zen Master's Dance

A GUIDE TO UNDERSTANDING

DŌGEN AND WHO YOU ARE

IN THE UNIVERSE

Jundo Cohen

Wisdom Publications
199 Elm Street
Somerville, MA 02144 USA
wisdomexperience.org

*Library of Congress Cataloging-in-Publication Data*

Names: Cohen, Jundo, author.
Title: The Zen master's dance: a guide to understanding Dōgen and
    who you are in the universe / Jundo Cohen.
Description: Somerville, MA, USA: Wisdom Publications, 2020. |
    Includes bibliographical references and index.
Identifiers: LCCN 2020007599 (print) | LCCN 2020007600 (ebook) |
    ISBN 9781614296454 (paperback) | ISBN 9781614296461 (ebook)
Subjects: LCSH: Dōgen, 1200–1253.
Classification: LCC BQ9449.D657 C64 2020 (print) |
    LCC BQ9449.D657 (ebook) | DDC 294.3/927092—dc23
LC record available at https://lccn.loc.gov/2020007599
LC ebook record available at https://lccn.loc.gov/2020007600

ISBN 978-1-61429-645-4    ebook ISBN 978-1-61429-646-1

24 23 22 21 20    5 4 3 2 1

Cover design by Graciela Galup. Interior design by James D. Skatges.
Cover photo by Ohmky on Unsplash.

*To all my Friends along the Way at Treeleaf Sangha*

# Contents

# Introduction

Eihei Dōgen, a Japanese Zen Master of long ago, heard the music of the universe that sounds as all events and places, people, things, and spaces. He experienced reality as a great dance moving through time, coming to life in the thoughts and acts of all beings. It is a most special dance, for it is the dance that the whole of reality is dancing, with nothing left out, that you and I are dancing, that is dancing as you and me. It is a vibrant, swirling, flowing, merging and emerging unity that Buddhists sometimes call "emptiness," as the motion and sweep of the dance "empties" us of the sense of only being separate beings, and fills and reaffirms us as the whole. We, as human beings, can't be sure when or where this dance began, or whether it even has a beginning or end. But we can come to see that it is being danced now in each step and breath we take, much as a dance unfolds and constantly renews with every turn or leap of its dancers.

You and I are dancers in this dance, as is every creature great or small, the mountains and seas, every grain of sand or massive galaxy, the atoms that make up the universe and the whole universe itself. Everything in reality, no matter how old or vast, no matter how unnoticed or small, is dancing this dance together. And although we may feel as if we are separate dancers—finite individuals on a grand stage spanning all of time and space—we are also the dance itself dancing through us. A universe of dancers that are being danced up in this dance that the whole universe is dancing.

Picture in your mind a spectator witnessing a dance so vigorous and vibrant that its countless actors seem to vanish in the swirl of motion: single dancers becoming pairs, then groups, coming together and separating moment by moment, yet so merged as the overall movement that, from a distance, individual dancers can no longer be seen. It is like single raindrops vanishing in a distant storm. The dance is the ground below, the air that's stirred, the light of moon and stars in the open sky above. We are such fragile drops in motion, but also the whole ground, the whole motion, every breath of air, the moon and all the stars, the entirety of sky that is dancing too—for the dance is the whole of everything. It's a dance that leaves nothing out.

Indeed, the swirling dance constantly spins out new shapes and creations, gives temporary form to each and all of the individual dancers. From this vantage point, each of us is no more solid or separate than eddies in swirling water, dust devils in the breeze, flashes of lighting casting momentary light and shadow, each there for a while before fading back into the dance. The dance of nature in motion seems to spin us out onto the stage, then spin us back in, giving the appearance of birth and death. But beyond those temporary appearances, we are also the whole dance itself—a dance which happens before, during, and after our limited sense of time. There are scenes during life of youth, health, love, joy, and beauty, as well as sickness and sorrow, violence and war. Yet all are outward appearances rippling across the surface of it all.

So united did Dōgen see that whole that, in his mind, each point holds all other points, near or far, each point miraculously fully contains the whole, and each moment of time ticks with all other moments of time, before or after. It is much like saying that every step of each dancer somehow embodies, depends upon, and also fully expresses every step by all the other dancers on the stage, past, present, or future, and fully contains the entire dance too. Dōgen experienced the time of the dance as the overall movement that is fully held and expressed in each individual move itself, with past not only flowing into present and future, but future flowing into the present and past, as the present fully holds the past and future of the dance.

Can we truly say that there are separate dancers in this all-encompassing dance? Endless dances are going on within each dancer, each cell and each atom, each bond and reaction, just dancing within and with each other . . . dancing within dancing. We can experience all dancers and all reality absolutely absorbed in the constant motion of the dance. As the borders that separate our sense of self from the rest of the world soften or drop away, we see that there is no dance outside, no "me" and "you" inside the dance. There is only that which flows from inside to outside, outside to in—all borders, all barriers dropped away and the whole having no surface or edge.

Please don't understand the concept of this dance merely intellectually. Instead, join in, truly feel what it is to be swept up in this dance as this dance. Master Dōgen spoke of practice, putting it all in motion. Where this dance has come from, where it is going, is not as important as the dance that is truly realized—made real—right here, in your next leap and gesture. The dance is always right underfoot, so just dance, without thought of any other place.

## How to Dance

What would a dance be without some dance lessons? Each dancer can find herself—find her identity in the dance knowing her life as a dance too (a personal dance within the great dance), and that her grace, balance, direction, the choices she makes in each step by step, help create the dance as she goes. In his many writings, Master Dōgen, our master instructor, shows us how to dance with skill and grace. His dance secrets come down to a few fundamentals:

The first step is no step, sitting upright and very still. This is zazen, seated Zen, in which we assume a balanced and stable posture, breathe deeply and naturally, and just sit. In this sitting, we let go of tangled thoughts and judgments as best we can. We try not to wallow in our emotions or get caught up in long trains of thought, but instead let things be. We sit in equanimity, beyond judging good or bad, with a sense that this sitting is the one and only act that needs to be done in this moment, the one place to be in the whole universe. We sit in the present instant without engaging thoughts of past or future, and in doing so, we encounter the timeless wholeness of just this moment. As we sit unmoving, the whole moving world flows past and through us. When we sit with the trust that nothing is lacking in zazen, our sitting is complete because we stop all other measuring.

We human beings are always chasing goals, feeling our lack, judging good and bad, and feeling friction between our wants and reality. But when we sit in *shikantaza*—in "just sitting that hits the mark"—we stop chasing goals for a time. Sitting is its own goal and completion. When we sit this way, the division between us and the world drops away and we feel the profound wholeness of the dance. That is the first lesson.

Master Dōgen's next lesson is the sacredness of all things and activities. Getting up from the sitting cushion, we return to a life of goals and tasks, work that needs tending, clothes that need mending. In his teachings, Master Dōgen said we should not separate life and practice, but instead see everything and all moments *as* sacred practice. Rising in the morning, using the toilet and washing, cleaning and cooking, are all steps in the dance. Every single thought, word, and gesture, no matter how seemingly ordinary and mundane, is sacred.

This does not mean that all our actions are equally good. We need to live and act in skillful ways in order to taste the overarching goodness and sacredness of life. Thus, Master Dōgen's next lesson tells us to always seek to do good and to avoid doing harm. By that he means that we should avoid greed, anger, jealousy, and other damaging mental states. We should live with balance, poise, and moderation. In our own thoughts, words, and acts, we should choose that which is free from such harmful behaviors. In turn, the lessons of zazen and Zen practice will help us to do this. Thus, dancing well leads us to practice as better dancers, while being better dancers allows us to dance well.

Of course, realizing this truth, getting it into our bones and living accordingly, is what our practice is about.

Except where noted, all translations in this book are by the author.

# How to Read Dōgen

Master Dōgen's legacy is contained in various writings and records, such as his *Shōbōgenzō*, the *Right Dharma Eye Treasury*. In them, he expresses the path of zazen and of diligent practice in all of life. Unfortunately, some say that Dōgen's way with words is hard to pierce, that his strings of wandering phrases can leave the reader lost. Whole books and hundreds of articles have been written seeking to explain what the old master was trying to say. Some people think his writing is just meaningless gobbledygook, or something so profound that only a Buddha can understand it.

I do not believe, however, that Dōgen is so hard to understand at all. I don't mean to say that his message is simple. It is multilayered, multifaceted, and subtle when not downright nebulous. So, in order to understand it, we must first study a considerable amount of Buddhist history and important Mahayana and Zen doctrines—as well as Dōgen's own unique perspectives on those doctrines—before we fathom where he is coming from. But beyond that, his original and imaginative writing style is really not such a mystery once we get used to his quirks and stylistic habits.

I think that the reason we sometimes get tangled up in Dōgen's writing is because we don't hear him as a musician playing a jam, a kind of wild and innovative "Zen jazz."

I have described Dōgen's sense of the world as evincing a great dance, and perhaps the best way to see that dance is as the fluid forms, open expression, and creativity of jazz or modern dance moving to creative sounds.

All beings and events move and merge in lively interactions that, while often chaotic on the surface, reveal a hidden unity below. Dōgen wished to teach his students how to move with grace and balance through that dance, and his words and writings sought to express that vision. His free dance emerged, however, from his training in classical dance forms, including traditional Mahayana Buddhism. It was not "do whatever you want" dancing, as some folks incorrectly imagine Zen to be. At heart, Dōgen was a classically trained artist and dancer honoring the refined choreography and rituals of monastic life. At the same time, he was willing to be wide-ranging, free, and experimental in his expression of those classical teachings. That is why it may be helpful to hear Dōgen's writings as the musical voicing of his dance, and thus to think of him as a classically trained jazz musician who, for all his wild sound, never left behind the basics of musical theory and conservatory training.

A modern jazz musician like saxophonist John Coltrane, by taking the basic melodies and themes of the standard score, by bending and turning them inside out, changing the beat and going to unchartered places, squeezes amazing sounds and fresh discoveries out of the well-worn original. The thing about appreciating Coltrane and many of the other jazz greats is to know that by their doing so, each player makes his own musical expression the same as, but different from, the standard tune it is based upon. Dōgen does the same in imaginatively re-expressing ancient teachings. Sometimes with Dōgen and Coltrane it is the sound, man, and the hinted implications, more than the straight meaning. People often get tangled in Dōgen's style because they constantly look for Dōgen's intellectual and philosophical meaning in every phrase. They shut the book in frustration or think that Dōgen was pulling the wool over people's eyes. However, although I believe that Dōgen *was* often trying to impress his listeners with a "hot" set of startling phrases, I don't think that he was ever just put-ting on a show. He said what he meant, and meant what he *felt*. Dōgen was being true to the Buddha's sound. With Dōgen, we have to learn to *feel* the music more than to intellectually understand the score.

It's not just Coltrane or jazz: Picasso and the other modern visual artists took the concrete image of a table, a human face, or a guitar and, by pulling apart the pieces and reassembling them in unexpected ways, led us to discover new insights into ordinary table-ness, face-icity, and guitar-ism. Hendrix explored guitar-ism in his own ways, by bending a Fender™ and having it do things that had never quite been done before. It is just the same for slamming poets or rap-pers, and modern DJs find it with a turntable and sampling old hits, spoken phrases, and random noises at a rave. T. S. Eliot and James Joyce did much the same with words, linking them together in unex-pected ways and with powerful effect. (I have heard it said that Joyce did not, himself, always know what he "meant" in his own writing, but he knew that something alive was emerging.) Some 700 or so years before these modern folks, Dōgen had the equivalent approach, taking "standard" Mahayana Buddhist teachings, fanciful but tradi-tional Buddhist images, and "samples" of quotes from well-known stories related to his intended topics, tearing them apart, and tossing all back together again, remixing them, in order to discover and un-cover new feelings, sounds, implications, visions, and wisdom, all in what was often pretty wild imagery to start with!

To me, Master Dōgen was "blowing his *Shōbōgenzō*-sax"—riffing, rockin', rollin', ranting, and roof-raising by expressing-folding-bending-fractalizing-unfolding-straightening-teasing-releasing the "standard tunes" of the *sutras* and old kōans. The untrained ear can't always make heads nor tails of the complex rhythms, flying notes, wild tempos—maybe sometimes even Dōgen himself could not grab hold of the animal he was creating—but I know that he felt what he meant, and that he knew that the creature he was fashioning had life.

Still, it would be a mistake to only listen to Dōgen's playful sound while forgetting the basic Buddhist doctrines he was exploring. For

example, in one of the earliest pieces in the *Shōbōgenzō*, Dōgen
commented on passages of the classic *Heart Sutra* that include the
term *prajñā* ("wisdom" in Buddhist lingo—a profound insight into
emptiness) and the realization of form as emptiness. Of these he wrote
the following (additions in brackets are mine, to highlight the Buddhist teachings tossed in the mix):

> When Bodhisattva Avalokiteśvara [Kannon, the Bodhi-
> sattva of Compassion] practices most profound *prajñā-
> pāramitā* [perfection of wisdom], the entire body
> manifests [a phrase apparently added by Dōgen not found
> in the original] that the five aggregates [in traditional
> Buddhism, these are the five factors or *skandhas* whose
> workings are said to account for our experience of reality]
> are empty.
>
> [Dōgen comments:] The five aggregates are form, feel-
> ing, perception, volition, and consciousness. These are five
> instances of prajñā. Seeing clearly is prajñā itself. To
> expound the principle of this teaching, it is that "form is
> emptiness and emptiness is form." [Dōgen then adds a line
> not found in the original *Heart Sutra*] Form is form, emp-
> tiness is emptiness. One hundred grasses [all phenomena]
> are such, the multiplicity of forms is such.

Next, Dōgen references emptiness as space:

> The [Indian] god Indra asks the venerable monk Subhūti,
> "Reverend One! When bodhisattvas, great beings, wish to
> study this profound prajñā-pāramitā, how should they study
> this?" Subhūti says, "[ . . . ] they should study such as space."

Dōgen intended the addition of the phrase "the entire body" and
the example of emptiness as space to interlace with the climax of the
essay, a poem on form and emptiness by Dōgen's own teacher, Master

Rujing (whom Dōgen often refers to as "the Old Buddha" in a gesture of tremendous respect):

*My late master, the Old Buddha, says:*
*Entire body like a mouth [of a windbell], hanging in space;*
*Unconcerned that the wind is east, west, south, or north . . .*

In these short passages we find many ideas and characters of Mahayana Buddhism indispensable to understanding what Dōgen is expressing: Bodhisattva Avalokiteśvara, prajñā-pāramitā, the five aggregates, the phrase "form is emptiness, emptiness is form," and other *Heart Sutra* references. We also find some standard Buddhist images, such as the description of phenomena as the "one hundred grasses." That is why a good grounding in traditional Buddhist, Mahayana, and Zen philosophy is vital to understanding Dōgen. In addition, we also benefit by knowing some Buddhist history in order to answer questions like, why does a Hindu god like Indra appear in a Buddhist text, who is Subhūti, and who was Dōgen's master, Rujing? Once we understand these references, we can then see how Dōgen is making creative contributions to the text.

In the end, however, the truths expressed in the *Heart Sutra* and Dōgen's commentary on it are not intended to be so much intellectually understood as "grokked" (science fiction author Robert A. Heinlein's term for such thorough understanding—whether by intuition or empathy—that the observer merges with and is reaffirmed by that which is understood).

Dōgen does not deviate from the classic Mahayana teaching that wisdom is the clear and free experience of the total identity and interpenetration of unbounded emptiness. This emptiness, which is actually a wholeness, manifests in all of the countless things of the world, as well as in the mental faculties that create our subjective experience of that world. But once Dōgen establishes this standard Buddhist melody, he picks up his horn and lets loose. Tossing all intellectual knowledge away, we get Dōgen's message by "digging the rhythms"—that is, the power, the feel of his words.

In another example, Dōgen wilds and re-wilds the already fantastically wild *Lotus Sutra*. In a famous scene in the text, a *stupa* (a traditional pavilion or tower containing the ashes or relics of a Buddha or other great Ancestor) thousands of miles tall emerges from the ground and comes to rest in midair. Buddha Śākyamuni sees that another Buddha, named Abundant Treasures, is sitting inside, and the two Buddhas share a seat within the tower and preach together. In an astonishing kind of metaphysical loop, all this is depicted as occurring in the sky over Vulture Peak, the Indian sacred site where the *Lotus Sutra* is being preached: a scene of the preaching of the very book that contains within it the preaching scene. It is already a pretty wild vision before Dōgen even sets to work on it. Here is the original:

> At this time, before the Buddha, a stupa of seven treasures [gold, silver, pearl, etc.], five hundred *yojanas* in height and two hundred and fifty yojanas in length and breadth, sprang up from the earth and abided in the sky . . . When that Buddha [Abundant Treasures] was practicing as a bodhisattva in the past, he deeply vowed: "After I have realized Buddhahood and died, if anywhere in the ten directions there is any place where the *Lotus Sutra* is being preached, my stupa shall spring out and appear in that place so that I may hear the sutra's preaching."

In a *Shōbōgenzō* essay called "Hokke-Ten-Hokke" (The Flower of Dharma Turns the Flower of Dharma), Dōgen takes this scene, flips it around, stirs it up, and brings it home. The expression "turning the flower of *Dharma*" can mean a Buddha's preaching of the Dharma, or Buddhist truth, which turning by the Buddha's flowery tongue expresses the whole beautiful turning universe that is itself like a flower turning:

[Dōgen says:] There is the turning of the flower of Dharma in the appearance "before the Buddha" of the "treasure stupa," which is a "height of five hundred yojanas." There is the turning of the flower of Dharma that is the "Buddha sitting inside the stupa," whose breadth is "two hundred and fifty yojanas." There is a turning of the flower of Dharma by springing forth from the earth and abiding in the earth, whereby mind is without obstructions and matter is without limits. There is the turning of the flower of Dharma in springing out of the sky and abiding in the earth, which is limited by the eyes and limited by the body.

Vulture Peak is within the stupa, and the treasure stupa is on Vulture Peak. The treasure stupa is a stupa of treasure abiding in space, and space opens space for the treasure stupa. The timeless Buddha within the stupa shares a seat with the Buddha of Vulture Peak, and the Buddha of Vulture Peak shares the realization of the Buddha within the stupa. When the Buddha of Vulture Peak experiences this state within the stupa together with body, mind, and all things, he also enters into the state of the turning of the flower of Dharma. [. . .] This "within the stupa," "before the Buddha," "the treasure stupa," and "space" are not limited to Vulture Peak; they are not limited to the realm of phenomena; they are not limited to some half-way stage; neither are they the whole world. Nor are they matters of some fixed "place in the Dharma." They are simply "non-thinking."

The sacred all and everything of this scene and all reality, so thoroughly interconnected and interflowing, every bit pouring in and out of every bit, is the turning of the flower of the Buddha's teaching, the whole universe turning, sometimes experienced in the world of restrictions and sometimes unrestricted. And all of it is the "non-thinking" (*hi-shiryō*) of zazen. (This reference is the same one that Dōgen often employs to describe the state of mind in which "thinking-not-thinking" is "non-thinking"—a state of wholeness and clarity in which we are untangled from thoughts in zazen.)

Sometimes we can clearly make out the original melody Dōgen was working with—a sutra passage, a poem, an old kōan. At other times, we can barely do so, for it is not always the case that Dōgen was trying to make a point through reasoned words, but that he wanted to communicate the sound and emotion of the music.

I think there are many passages—like Dōgen's above commentary on the *Lotus Sutra*—where even he did not know the terrain to which the sound had carried him or what it meant in intellectual terms. I will go so far as to say that perhaps from time to time he backed himself into a musical corner, so that he was not always sure where he had ended up or how to get out of that spot—except by jumping in deeper. For some reason we assume that every word Dōgen wrote has an intellectually concrete meaning, as opposed to it merely expressing a *feeling* of truth. Nonetheless, I believe that Dōgen profoundly recognized the message that these true feelings evoked.

## And Thus This Book

In the pages that follow I will introduce that standard "songbook" of Mahayana Buddhism where it is appropriate to understand the source of Dōgen's teachings, and also point out where I think he was just jammin' on his horn. In many places I have tried to experiment, offering my interpretation of Dōgen's words, seeking to walk the fine line between explaining Dōgen's doctrinal ideas and conveying the simple feeling I think he was shooting for.

As I have mentioned, some writers and Dōgen scholars take a highly philosophical approach to understanding his teachings, and such explanations sometimes run the risk of becoming too analytical, turning the subtleties of Dōgen's writing and speaking style into intellectual ideas that are excessively complex and tangled. On the other hand, some writers, coming from a worshipful and religious attitude,

have tried to turn Dōgen into a mysterious oracle whose strange proc-
lamations can only be understood by those who have attained some
otherworldly, transcendent enlightenment. Dōgen's harder passages
are portrayed as cryptic, even magical words that cannot be grasped
by the ordinary or unenlightened mind. I don't agree. There is a logic
to Dōgen. His teachings derive from traditional Mahayana sources
such as the Perfection of Wisdom literature and Nagarjuna's Madhya-
maka philosophy, which explores the implications of the fact that all
phenomena are empty of independent self-existence; the *Huayan* or
*Flower Garland Sutra* teachings, which state that all phenomena flow
and interpenetrate each other and the totality of reality; sutras like
the *Lotus Sutra* and other texts that offer a variety of teachings and
parables that became seeds for Dōgen's inspiration; perspectives on
Buddha Nature and original enlightenment, which state that all of us
sentient beings are already Buddha, already enlightened—although
our ignorance and unskillful behavior keeps this fact hidden from us;
and much more. For that reason, "Dōgen logic" is rather different
from our ordinary, common-sense way of experiencing the world. Yet
it is a logic nonetheless, and it can be explained in generally understandable terms even to people new to Buddhist teachings.

For example, in our ordinary experience of life, a mountain is not a
cup of tea, and neither a mountain nor a cup of tea are you or me. A is
not B, and neither one is C nor D. However, for Mahayana teachers
like Dōgen, mountains are mountains and also cups of tea. Tiny teacups hold great mountains within, as well as the whole world and all
of time. Mountains quench our thirst, mountains walk and preach
the Dharma, and mountains are also other faces of you and me. It is
not merely that our ordinary eyes might see a nearby mountain reflected on the liquid inside a cup, or painted on its side, or reflected
like a kaleidoscope in each poured drop, but that the mountain and
the whole universe is truly poured and held in every drop of tea to be
tasted, and is contained in the cup itself. The teacup, though held in
our hands, is also huge, boundless, as big as a mountain and the whole
universe. The whole universe is just a great vessel which is also the

vessel in our hands—a vessel that cradles our hands as we cradle it. (If this is hard to get your mind around, it is fine to approach it in a poetic sense until, on the zazen cushion, one can actually realize such truths.)

When we drink tea, as it enters our mouth and we taste it on our tongue and it merges with our body, we too enter the tea, are tasted by and merge with it. Likewise, in drinking tea we enter the mountains and the whole universe. The tea swallows us as we swallow the tea, and the mountain/universe drinks us as we drink the mountain/universe— all in the simple action of tasting a cup of tea. The tea steeps all time and space as you steep tea; the mountain pours the universe as the universe moves with your hands when pouring a cup. Each drop of tea, each inch of the mountain or atom of the universe glitters as a unique and precious jewel, each unique and whole unto itself, yet each is also the all. That is the kind of world vision that Dōgen is usually expressing.

This is why many translators rightly declare that it is hard to render Dōgen into English or other languages. One can trace his grammar fairly closely but then end up losing or stepping over much of his wit with homonyms and synonyms, intentionally misread Chinese characters, newly created words, and scrambled sentences, imaginatively reinterpreted classic quotes, puns, and double-triple-quadruple entendres, fancy rhythms, and wild poetic riffs. One also struggles to identify the many quips, story citations, and quotes of well-known or obscure texts—some now forgotten—that were Dōgen's musical grab bag. However, that does not mean that diving into the *Shōbōgenzō*— like developing an ear for John Coltrane or T. S. Eliot or an eye for Picasso—isn't worth the effort.

We sometimes say in the Zen world: hear with the eyes, see with the ears. Rather than trying to intellectually understand every word of Dōgen's, we can feel his tune and rise up to dance with life *as* life— with every atom, tea drop, mountain, and star in the sky.

What Dōgen wrote so long ago—the lessons contained in his wild words and music—is as relevant to students today as it was 800 years ago. In his writings, we have the talks that Dōgen delivered to his monks, and often to laypeople. Because his advice can be so helpful and vital even today, and because his path of zazen goes beyond time, his words speak directly to you and me today. The great differences of culture separating ancient Japan from the modern world and the span of so many centuries can be forgotten as Dōgen conveys his timeless insights that transcend here and there, now and then. This is how we are guided by Dōgen's great teachings and his ability to experience the ordinary things of this world as sacred. Thus we come to see that there is beauty and wholeness in this universe that transcends and holds all of the ugliness and broken pieces. The key to this way of seeing is the practice of zazen, just like music and dance pull together and are embodied through practice.

## Dōgen's Musical Themes

This is a book about learning to hear Dōgen's music and to dance the universe's accompanying dance. In the pages that follow, I will try to explain some of this wise-wild, straight-when-bent yet bent-when-straight Zen logic that I believe Dōgen was expressing, and I will try to do so in understandable terms with the best examples I can muster.

A few key Dōgenesque ideas will pop up again and again, so it's worth mentioning them here:

First is zazen, sitting not merely as a means or tool to attain some experience or state of enlightenment, but as the sitting of enlightenment itself. It is a sitting-for-sitting's-sake view in which sitting is free of all thought of before and after, process or goal. Zazen is a sacred, whole activity fulfilled by sitting itself.

Next, we must come to affirm all our activities in life as sacred rituals, even when we don't necessarily see or realize them as such. For Dōgen, scratching our noses, washing a window, or caring for a sick friend are all the whole universe scratching, washing, and caring for the whole universe. Dōgen teaches us how to see life in these terms.

He also constantly reminds us to behave with poise and balance, and to be free of excess desire, anger, jealousy, and other divided thinking. Instead he emphasizes moderation, simplicity, peace, help-fulness, and kindness. If we live harshly, the world will appear harsh and harmful things will result. If we live in a gentle way, the world will appear with greater clarity and good effects will result from our actions.

But in order to understand this, we have to get on our sitting cush-ion and personally realize these ways of experiencing life. In zazen, dropping thoughts and categories, we encounter the interflowing and penetrating wholeness of it all, the place where Buddha and Dōgen live—and you and I too—for they all interflow and penetrate us. Then, getting up from the sitting cushion, we seek to embody the sacredness, poise, balance, and goodness that Dōgen saw in every act. This is his vision of continuous "practice-enlightenment" in which every Buddha-like thought, word, or act brings Buddha to life in that moment.

Of those writings of Dōgen's that we will dance through in these pages, the first centers on the sitting of zazen itself: "Fukan Zazengi" (The Way of Zazen Recommended to Everyone) is Dōgen's ode to zazen and a how-to manual on the practice of *shikantaza*, "just sit-ting." This essay is followed by Master Dōgen's most concise introduc-tion to his key views of the world—including his "viewless views," which transcend viewer and viewed. In "Genjō Kōan" (Realizing the Truth Right Here), written as a letter to a lay student, Dōgen waxes on about his vision of the interpenetration of the relative and abso-lute, the moon of enlightenment that shines as all things, and the con-cept of continuous practice that fans the wind of ever-present enlight-enment. "Zanmai-O-Zanmai" (Samādhi That Is the King of Samādhis) is Dōgen's special view of Zen *samādhi*, a unified mind, as present right here, right now, in the sacred sitting of zazen.

Next we will explore Dōgen's view of all things, all time, all life and death, dancing in and dancing as each other as a single whole. "Ikka Myōju" (One Bright Pearl) is a tribute to the wholeness of this world manifesting in the precious and complete, shining jewel of zazen. "Uji" (Being-Time) states that there is much more to time than our ceaseless rush into the future. "Shōji and Zenki" (Life and Death, and the Whole Works) are two short pieces on the practice of living and dying with all of one's heart and realizing life as the "whole works."

In all these writings, Dōgen seeks to shine a light on aspects of the great dance. My task will be to shine a spotlight on Dōgen's colorful show.

In a few of these sections—such as my presentations of "Genjō Kōan" and "Fukan Zazengi"—I have on occasion significantly modernized and adjusted the original wording. I have also added my own commentary to help the reader understand Dōgen's main points. Since these two essays are often singled out as the most basic introduction to Dōgen's views (they were supposedly intended as guidance to lay followers), I thought it would be good to try this experiment with these writings and a few other sections. I have tried to point out the chapters and passages where I've changed Dōgen's language, but readers wishing to compare my version with some of the more common translations can find several readily available online and in print. I have listed these in the appendix of sources at the end of this book.

For the other sections of this book, I have developed English translations that more closely track Dōgen's original Japanese and are not unlike other widely accepted modern translations available today, including those by my own teacher, Gudo Wafu Nishijima Roshi, and his student, Chodo Cross. I worked simultaneously from the original in period Japanese as well as modernized Japanese versions. In addition, a variety of modern English translations provided suggested wording. Based on all these, I developed, phrase by phrase, a translation that I felt best conveyed Dōgen's meaning. While I have tried to follow Dōgen's words as closely as possible, I also advise readers to take my presentation as an interpretation of what I think Dōgen likely meant, instead of a strictly literal translation. Maybe all of the widely used modern translations are little more than interpretations of Dōgen's wild side. Thus, a committed student of Dōgen is best advised to read my own text alongside one or more of the respected English translations.

I sometimes quip, with a grain of salt, that this book is "a definitive guide" to reading Dōgen. The reason I call it *a* rather than *the* definitive guide is simple. While I believe that my presentations of Dōgen's teachings are true and faithful to his intent and will give the reader a thorough understanding of what the old master was trying to convey in his writings, I am not so egotistical as to claim that my insights are the last word. Others may disagree with my interpretations and will have their own opinions regarding Dōgen's meaning. But only Dōgen truly knew what he felt and meant. I can only let my interpretation stand on its own and ask readers to judge for themselves whether it aligns with Dōgen's teachings.

In the end, the heart of Dōgen's words must be realized in our zazen and in the continuous practice of practice-enlightenment on and off the cushion. This is where the dance is truly danced.

# The Way of Zazen Recommended for Everyone

FUKAN ZAZENGI

Life's dance takes unexpected turns.

I am writing this some weeks after receiving an esophageal and stomach cancer diagnosis. The doctors are optimistic, but they won't know the real prognosis until they do surgery a few days from now. Like many twists and turns in life, this news came as quite a surprise to me. In general, I'm doing okay with it, but I am also afraid sometimes, as we humans often are when faced with our mortality. I don't want to pretend that I am some kind of hero who is beyond all fear. I am not. I'm a complete Zen coward! I believe that some level of fear is hardwired into the deepest parts of our brains, and it awakens when we ponder our own sickness and death.

But that's okay, because it's not the end of the story.

Another part of me is beyond all fear. I mean that. Part of me is afraid but part of me is not afraid at all. It's the part of me that is wonderfully beyond "me," beyond all fear of death—an aspect of my being that is fine with whatever happens. The part of me that knows there is no place to fall to and that does not believe in death in the usual way we think about it. I feel content, even though I am also worried about my upcoming surgery. There are serious risks, and the operation might not work. I want to get the cancer out, but the treatment is painful and without guarantees. I am afraid, and sometimes the fear makes me sweat from head to toe. I realize I may not be here in a year or two, or even months from now. I may not be here tomorrow. What will become of my family? I miss my kids, my wife, the cat. Who will teach my daughter to ride a bike, or show my son how to shave? Sometimes the loneliness I feel makes me cry at night.

At the same time, I am beyond all fear, and there is not the least re-sistance to death in my heart. Through Zen practice, I stopped being concerned about death a long time ago. If death comes, let it come. Whatever happens, I'm willing to dive right in. Thus, I am content to be here in this hospital room. All is as it should be and I overflow with joy. An amazing aspect of Zen, the essence of the wisdom and compas-sion at its very center, is that it allows all such feelings to be true at once, each in its own way. Each perspective has its place, and there is not the least bit of conflict among ideas and emotions that at first appear to be contradictory.

I would like to tell you where this strength comes from—it comes from zazen and Dōgen's way of shikantaza. These are my source of courage today. This wondrous Zen practice gives me strength and ac-ceptance, and it has done so over the decades that I have practiced it. Because of this path, I can accept whatever is in store for me in the coming weeks and beyond, even as I stare into the face of my fear. Oh, it's true that it is not so easy to sit zazen some days when the mind seems swept with storms of worry, thoughts of "what if." Sometimes our heads and hearts can become so filled with dark thoughts and painful emotions that we find it nearly impossible to sit still. Our doubts and struggles make us want to distract ourselves, or run away. I know. It can be true even for old hands at this practice.

But I want to encourage all of us to sit nonetheless and to bring this practice off the sitting cushion too. Master Dōgen's way of sitting is called shikantaza zazen. As Master Dōgen describes it, shikantaza is very simple: we sit in total acceptance of what is, dropping judgments and resistance to all of life's happenings during the time of sitting. Equanimity is vital. I like to say that it is sitting in such equanimity that we even feel equanimous about not feeling "equanimity" sometimes. Thus, I accept even those days of sitting, or life, when my heart is not so peaceful. I honor even those times when I am downright scared. I am at peace and content with not always needing to feel "peaceful and content" all the time, like some days when sitting zazen in this cancer ward bed.

While sitting, we put aside any other plans or concerns. Our one plan and concern is to sit. We let the world just be the world, our struggles just be our struggles, our fears just be our fears. We don't try to change things or do anything at all but just sit. We sit with a subtle faith and trust that the sitting itself is all we need to do while sitting; it's a complete act, the one place to be and the one thing necessary in that moment. During zazen, we drop all resistance or feeling of lack, letting the act of sitting be enough in itself. Such total allowance is how we ordinary beings can manifest some of the wisdom and peace of a Buddha in our hearts.

Sitting in radical equanimity, we let all of life be just what it is and our resistance drops away. Whether it's cancer, problems at work or in a marriage, our broken dreams or dashed hopes—all the ups and downs of life are "just as they are" when we are sitting. Our problems and fears remain but, somehow, by dropping resistance to them, everything is okay. We let them be, we leave them behind, in our equanimity during the minutes of our sitting. (Of course, after sitting we had best work to fix that marriage, solve the problems, cure our cancer. However, during the minutes of sitting, we put aside all need to fix, solve, and cure.) By assuming a balanced, stable, and comfortable physical posture—as comfortable as our bodies or health will allow—we facilitate a balanced, stable, and easy heart. Then, we just let be.

Zazen doesn't have to be complicated. We don't have to run after bliss or try to make ourselves feel peaceful. Rather, we can just give up the fight and rest in the peace that is equanimity itself. For trying to feel joy and peace is hard, but knowing the joy of acceptance and the peace of putting down the fight is relatively easy and, in the end, more effective. Our problems, sadness, and fear become small or fade away when we simply let life be life. This is what the Buddha himself found when he sat under the bodhi tree and attained enlightenment.

Long ago, Śākyamuni Buddha tried all kinds of practices and all manner of intense meditations in order to find true peace and wholeness in his heart. He tried deep meditations leading to radically altered states of consciousness. He pursued philosophical and intellectual understanding. He even starved himself, trying to punish his body in order to find freedom. But then, one day, after all those many years of effort, the Buddha-to-be sat cross-legged under a tree. He saw the simplicity and completeness of the morning star rising naturally on the distant horizon and gave up all fighting, striving, and resistance. He realized that the star, the world, and himself were just what they were, whole and complete. In that moment, he was freed of the need to fight or to run toward his desires and away from his aversions. He put aside all judgments and accepted the world on its own terms. In doing so, the hard borders and feelings of separation and alienation between him and all of life softened and dropped away. Thus he experienced an abiding wholeness and peace. He remained in this world with all its divisions, complications and troubles, yet also saw through them into wholeness.

We human beings have forgotten how to simply sit still, how to be whole and content while doing such a plain thing. Trees just stand, mountains sit still, even my little cat knows how to rest when she rests. Instead, we always run around trying to fill the holes in our hearts. We buy things, or we look for sex and love, success or fame, and other temporary distractions from our pain. Shikantaza, as "just sitting," teaches us to experience life in that unadulterated way.

Shikantaza is so radically "goalless," that it is often said to not be a method of meditation. So what is the "non-method" of shikantaza? There are several vital points:

## The Basics and the Missing Ingredient

Most experienced modern teachers of shikantaza agree on the basic points: you should sit in the lotus posture (or in some other stable posture such as Burmese, kneeling in *seiza*, or in a chair, as many modern students do), focus on the breath or the body as a place to rest the attention, or just be "openly aware" by letting your thoughts flow without grabbing onto them. While sitting in shikantaza, do not judge the experience of sitting or the circumstances you find yourself in. If you are caught in trains of thought, return to the breath, or the posture, or a feeling of spaciousness.

Sit daily for ten, twenty, thirty minutes or longer, but without any objective or need for reward. Do not seek special states of deep concentration or any unusual mental experiences. In fact, do not seek anything from zazen at all—whether that's enlightenment or becoming Buddha. Just sit!

These points are all correct. However, I sometimes feel that there is one more vital ingredient that we teachers should emphasize. In my view, by leaving out this point, some descriptions of shikantaza can miss the mark of Dōgen's conception of zazen. In his effusive descriptions of the specialness of zazen that appear in the "Fukan Zazengi," Dōgen did not leave us just sitting there like bumps on a log. By not placing one more fact front and center—or by leaving it out altogether—we modern teachers rob zazen of its power, turning it into a fire without its heat or a tiger without its claws.

What is this missing piece of the puzzle?

As mentioned before, we must sit shikantaza with the profound trusting that sitting itself is a complete and sacred act, the one and only action that need be done in that moment of sitting. As we shall see in the "Fukan Zazengi" and in Dōgen's other writings on zazen, this was Dōgen's unique point, and he emphasized it time and time again in his teachings. Zazen is all the Buddhas and Ancestors sitting in our own moment of sitting, as if our sitting turns us into those Buddhas and Ancestors on the spot. We must have faith in that fact. We must taste vibrantly that the mere act of sitting zazen is whole and complete, the total fruition of life's goals, with nothing lacking and nothing added to the bare fact of sitting here and now. No matter how busy our lives or how strongly we may feel tempted to be elsewhere, for the time of sitting we put aside all other concerns. To do this, we must have a sense that the single act of crossing the legs as Dōgen instructed (or sitting in some other balanced posture, as many modern students do) is the realization of all we've ever sought. That is why there is simply no other place to go in the world, nothing else to do besides sit in this posture.

Even if we do not yet fully believe in the completeness of zazen, we can nonetheless have trust and faith in it, and that trust and faith will soon turn into an actual experience. A friend who is a Broadway performer and Zen practitioner once told me that the "non-method" of zazen is like the case of a method actor playing the part of Willie Loman in *Death of a Salesman*. First the actor merely pretends he is Willie but eventually comes to embody Willie from head to toe. So, if needed, we sit zazen in the role of a totally satisfied and equanimous Buddha until Buddha comes to life for us.

Some scholars have pointed out that Dōgen's zazen has aspects of an esoteric Buddhist practice: do one action thoroughly, assume the form of Buddha in body, mind, and heart, and you come to embody Buddha in body, mind, and heart.

Unfortunately, we modern teachers do not always sufficiently emphasize this sacred, complete fulfillment of just sitting. I have sometimes witnessed zazen explained to newcomers like this: "Just sit in an upright posture, let your thoughts go, just breathe." I have heard the advice to students to "just follow the breath," or "straighten the back," or "don't grab onto thoughts," or "drop all goals," all of which are right and good, but few teachers say something like: "Sit zazen with the conviction that sitting is all that is needed in life," or, "Sit trusting that this sitting is the total fulfillment of all the universe," or, "Sit with a subtle sense that, were you to die right now on the cushion, sitting alone would have made a complete life." This is the kind of tone that Master Dōgen takes in "Fukan Zazengi" and elsewhere.

However, we should not think about or voice this truth of the completeness of zazen during zazen, but we must silently and subtly feel it deep down. Our feelings of lack or dissatisfaction will drop away in the wholeness and equanimity of sitting. Thus, I sometimes describe zazen as a "non-self"-fulfilling prophecy because, when we feel that sitting is complete, it *is* complete. On the other hand, if we feel that our zazen is incomplete, then it is incomplete. Zazen is just zazen, life is just life, but our judgment is subjective. How we see zazen is entirely up to us. But if we can know it as complete, we can do the same with all of life.

## A Most Special State

In many forms of Buddhist meditation, the purpose of sitting is to attain samādhi—a deep state of concentration—or other extraordinary states of consciousness. Dōgen felt that true samādhi is the act of sitting within wholeness without need for anything else. That does not mean that we don't experience deep states of concentration or other transcendent or eye-opening insights in shikantaza, but we neither run toward nor away from them. In fact, most of our difficult emotions like anger, frustration, and disappointment arise from our need to grasp what we desire or fight what we detest. In Dōgen's shikantaza we just sit as what is.

I sometimes compare shikantaza to the children's puzzle of Chinese finger cuffs, which are escaped not by forceful effort, but by non-resistance. Likewise, by dropping the hunt for enlightenment, by allowing everything to rest in the complete wholeness and acceptance of just sitting, by quenching all thirst in the sheer satisfaction of sitting alone, we realize a freedom and way of being that otherwise eludes us in this world of endless grasping and avoiding. By giving up the chase, we encounter enlightenment itself.

Many modern practitioners believe that shikantaza is just a way to get untangled from thoughts, or to feel some degree of balance, or to develop concentration, or to gain peace and clarity. (Shikantaza includes all those things, but also so much more.) Some take too literally the admonition that "just sitting is all there is" without sufficient understanding of the need for the body to resonate with the awareness that just sitting is all there could ever be or need be in the whole universe! Please do not think of shikantaza as identical to ordinary forms of meditation. Shikantaza is the most powerful and wonderful of states when we taste it as the only power that we need, and with it, embrace all the wonder of the universe.

## Letting Thoughts Go

Another vital aspect of shikantaza is to "let thoughts go." So the practice is, when you find yourself tangled up in thoughts, return your attention to open, spacious awareness, or to the breath as it enters and exits your body, or to your posture. Drop away your judgments of good and bad. Sit beyond judgments, without grabbing onto thoughts that flit through your mind.

According to tradition, the mind in zazen is like a clear mirror and the open blue sky. A mirror reflects whatever is placed before it— beautiful or ugly, friend or foe, welcome or detested—and allows each thing to be exactly what it is without rejection, resistance, preference, or judgment. The blue sky represents the open, clear, boundless, illuminated mind. Clouds represent thoughts. When clouds do appear, we simply allow them to drift by without trying to hold on to them, because when we do get caught, we make the mind even cloudier. Thus, to the extent that we can, we sit in the clear, bright open sky between the clouds, our mind untroubled.

In just sitting like this, something beautiful may result: the light, open clarity of the sky may shine through the occasional passing clouds, and we may realize that sky and clouds are not two. It is as if the light shines through the clouds and lightens them. If a problem drifts into my mind—like my cancer, for example—the light, open clarity of the sky shows me that it is not such a big problem after all, the heaviness of the problem lessens or vanishes, and silence and illumination fill everything. What seemed to be a dark, solid storm cloud suddenly appears as bright and permeable as lace. I believe this is what Dōgen meant when he spoke of "non-thinking" (hi-shiryō) or "thinking-not-thinking" (sometimes rendered as "beyond thinking"). The thought of the problem may remain, yet also not, both together.

Of course, on some days our minds will be so busy that the clouds completely block the sky. In those cases, what do we do? First, we return to following the breath or focusing on the posture, until the clouds clear a bit. If that does not work, then we simply observe our strong emotions or anxious thoughts, treating them like passing weather clouds. We just let the storm blow through without getting swept away. We can feel equanimity even about not feeling equanimous. A moment of zazen is a moment of light shining, seen or unseen, but shining clearly in the heart.

At the same time, "letting thoughts go" means not giving in to our worst feelings and letting them run unchecked. If we sit still, complacent, wallowing in our ignorance, anger, or jealousy, then we are not truly letting things be. Instead we are playing with and being pulled in by our thoughts. By not letting the powerful or negative emotions grab us, we rob them of much of their power and by not playing their game, we refuse to make things worse. We witness our inner storms like the parent of a child whose tantrum we cannot seem to still. Sometimes we just have to wait calmly for the child to tire and quiet down on her own, offering a loving smile and embrace while waiting patiently. If instead we get pulled into the situation, yelling and feeling miserable about the miserable state, we will throw more fuel on the fire, making it burn even hotter. Thus, "letting thoughts go" means letting things be, but it also refers to the cultivation of equanimity that does not slide into wallowing or stewing.

## Zazen Is Good for Nothing

Sitting in zazen gives us the ability to be at rest with whatever life tosses our way, to realize the preciousness and wholeness of life in this moment. How tragic if we instead turn our zazen into one more battle for achievement; a race to get to some peaceful place, grab some craved prize, or receive a spiritual reward. How unfortunate if we use zazen as a break from life, as a form of escape, never tasting the wholeness and completeness of life that shikantaza offers. If we fall into such traps, zazen becomes just one more expression of the rat race with a prize that is ever out of reach.

A famous Zen master, Kodo Sawaki, once said, "What's zazen good for? Absolutely nothing! This 'good for nothing' has got to sink into your flesh and bones until you actually practice what is truly good for nothing. Until then, your zazen is just good for nothing."[1]

But isn't zazen a great waste of time, then? Some of us get confused when we hear that shikantaza is not really meditation, that this practice has "no goal," and that we should give up trying to obtain anything from it. Talk of there being nothing to attain or the uselessness of zazen may falsely lead students to think that there is no value in sitting; that it is a waste of time rather than a state beyond all time and measure. Yet, on the contrary, not having anything to attain and not trying to get anything out of our zazen reminds us that the attainment of zazen is zazen itself. This is the missing ingredient of zazen.

When we truly taste to the marrow the real meaning of "nothing to achieve," we finally reach a great spiritual achievement. As counterintuitive as it sounds, resting in stillness without needing to run is, in fact, truly getting somewhere. If we wish to know the realm in which a Buddha feels fully at home in peace and acceptance, then the best way is to sit as a Buddha sits, totally at home in peace and acceptance.

Then, rising from our cushions, we may experience the world in a new way. We bring the stillness and wholeness of our shikantaza practice into the motion and calamity of life.

Getting on with our busy day, a part of us is now beyond goals. Despite all the work to do and achieve, we know there is ultimately nothing to do or achieve, yet each moment gives us the opportunity to put this "Zen mind" into practice in life—to live in each moment with gentleness, grace, sincerity, and ease. This is what Master Dōgen meant when he referred to continuous practice-enlightenment. It is one of the central messages in his "Fukan Zazengi," written for all of us.

## And So, "The Way of Zazen Recommended for Everyone"

The "Fukan Zazengi," a letter that Dōgen wrote setting out the fundamentals of zazen, might be thought of as his beginning instructions for his zazen dance. It is in this essay that the flawlessness of just sitting amid this flawed world becomes crystal clear.

The following translation is inspired by the fine work of many earlier translators into English, including that of my teacher, Nishijima Gudo Wafu, and his student, Chodo Cross. However, I've modernized Dōgen's tone here and there for better understanding by modern people and phrased some expressions freely to convey the implied meaning. Any mistakes I've made in doing so are all my own.

> When we examine it, the Buddha's truth is originally all around, complete, and all-pervading, so why would it depend on our practicing and realizing this fact?

What is the source of Dōgen's question? According to traditional biographies, as a young monk Dōgen believed in a teaching common in the Tendai school of Buddhism where he was then training. It said that all of us are already somehow Buddha, already fundamentally enlightened. The word "Buddha" refers to the flawless quality of our nature, the sense that there is nothing to add or take away, and not a single defect in need of fixing.

Mahayana Buddhists often use this word "Buddha" as a term for the truth of everything. But please don't get caught up in labels or ideas about what kind of "thing" Buddha is. When you freeze it into an idea and paste a name on it, you might forget how all-pervading this truth is. If we must try to explain it, Buddha might be said to be this world and life when we put aside all judgments and mental categories, names and labels. All those names, categories, and ideas create a separation between us and the rest of the world. This is what we Buddhists call "delusion." Buddha then means seeing beyond all those divisions, putting aside all our considerations about the world. And when we do so, what remains is not an empty vacuum, but rather a wholeness, a flowing dance that sweeps up everything that is this world, and sweeps us up too. It is wondrous, peaceful, and whole, even in the face of all the ups and downs, sickness and health, life and death of this world. To see that fact is what we call enlightenment.

This Buddha is what you and I truly are. Dōgen had great faith in this fact. But if that is the case, it also left him with a conundrum. If we are already Buddha, then why do we need to practice? Dōgen wondered. It was a real dilemma.

> The ultimate vehicle is free and present naturally, so why put forth great efforts to attain it? Furthermore, the whole entirety far transcends delusion, and all the dust and dirt we see in this world. So why be concerned with eliminating the latter, sweeping and polishing to uncover it? It is never apart from this very place; so why wander here and there to practice and search for it?

If it is completely present where we are, of what use are practice and enlightenment? The answer for Dōgen, as we shall see, was that unless we practice, the obvious is hidden to us, and what is present does not appear. Buddha and this chaotic world are not two. We can come to realize that all the things of life, you and me, and all the ideas we call delusion are actually Buddha too. Our practice is to see how the wholeness of Buddha is present even when not obvious to us. Zazen is one doorway that can lead us into that truth, but we have to give up all thought of Buddha in some distant time or place. We must trust that the tragedy, the ugliness we see, is like a dream, a performance on a stage—so is the beauty and joy. The performance is real to those of us living it, yet at the same time, it is not fully real; there is something more to it, something behind the scenes of division and strife. Buddha is present, though hidden to our clouded eyes.

> However, if there is but a hair's breadth gap, the separation is as wide as between heaven and earth; and if a trace of disparity or preference arises, the mind becomes lost in confusion.

In "Dream within a Dream," Dōgen said that although everything is a dream, it is our dream. Thus we had best see through it and dream it well. Sometimes the dream is not to our liking, sometimes it can seem like a nightmare, but Buddha is the dreamer and the dream too. When we wake up, we can see through those same dreams. But in order to realize this in our zazen and our lives, we must drop all thought of the least separation between us and Buddha from our minds. Otherwise Buddha will seem a million miles out of reach.

Dōgen also warns us that this realization is not a stagnant knowing, a final stopping place, but is instead a realization that keeps unfolding:

> Some people are proud of their understanding, puff up their achievements, and think that they are richly endowed with some realization of the Buddha's wisdom because of passing states of insight. They think that they have attained the ultimate, reached the truth, illuminated their minds, and gained the power to pierce the sky and touch the

heavens. But in fact, they have barely gotten their foot in the door, are lost in mental fantasies, are still missing the vital path of total emancipation.

A reason that we sit zazen is to sense this truth of no separation to the marrow of our being. Some people, having had some kind of mystical experience or opening in their zazen, spend the rest of their lives chasing after it, hoping that it will recur. They are sadly distracted from what is right before them. They might experience wholeness beyond this world of separation, but miss the presence of wholeness inherent right in this world of separation. Thus, it is only partial insight, not enlightenment. Seated zazen is just the beginning of practice. We must bring whatever insights and wisdom that arise during zazen off the cushion into our lives—right in this world of separation.

We can still see the traces of the Buddha Śākyamuni sitting for six years to manifest wisdom, and Bodhidharma faced the wall for nine years at Shao-lin temple to transmit this tradition. As the ancient sages were like that already: how could people today fail to practice zazen?

Seated zazen is a practice for us to realize truth. But we also have to bring this truth into the rest of our lives. It was so for Śākyamuni Buddha some 2,500 years ago in India. It was also true for Bodhidharma, the legendary figure who is said to have taken zazen to China from India, and to have sat in a cave for nine years. Each of these men practiced for a long time before they realized the truth, and they continued to sit all their lives after that. Practice throughout their life centered on zazen. Thus, it should be the same for all of us. Dōgen celebrates these great masters' continuous sitting with these words:

Therefore we should pause from the intellectual pursuit of studying ideas and chasing words and letters. We should learn the backward step of turning the light to illuminate from within. When we do so, body and mind will naturally drop away, and our original face will manifest.

Zazen entails turning the light of our attention inward. There are times in life for thinking and study, but also times to put the thoughts and analyzing down. When we do this, we may find that the sense of separation between us and the rest of the world begins to fade, "body and mind will naturally drop away," and our experience of our "original face" will manifest. This original face is another image for Buddha, that state in which all categories, judgments, and ideas of separation drop away:

> If you wish to attain suchness, you should immediately practice suchness. Now, in general, it is desirable to have a quiet room for practicing zazen. You should be moderate in eating and drinking.

"Suchness" is a sense of wholeness and simplicity pervading all reality, and Dōgen instructs us on the best way to experience suchness by practicing zazen. He gives us specific instructions on how to do this—the setting, the clothes we should wear, the position of our legs, and so on. It is good to sit in a quiet space, neither too dark nor too bright, not too hot or cold. Being in a quiet, sedate place helps the mind to calm and settle. We seek to sit in a good location, in a stable and balanced way, to facilitate the experience of the mind free of divisions. Notice that the environment, the body, and the mind all have a role to play; they are all part of this one action of knowing suchness.

However, in fact, we should really be able to sit zazen almost anywhere, because this practice is truly about sitting with what is without judgment or rejection. It is said that Dōgen sat on a ship in a terrible typhoon, during an earthquake, and when he was sick in bed. I myself have sat next to a busy highway, in the middle of a stinking garbage dump, in an airplane going through a storm, in a hospital emergency room with my sick child, at a noisy construction site, and during earthquakes and hurricanes after taking shelter. Now I sit in this cancer ward. The ultimate quiet space is between the ears, and if the mind is undisturbed, then there is nothing to disturb us. I often sit in places that are not quiet.

At Treeleaf Zendo in Japan, during our morning zazen we can hear birds chirping in the surrounding trees . . . but on occasion also a truck or car rushing down the nearby road, carpenters banging on a neighbor's roof, or a military helicopter passing overhead. These sounds have become one of my most powerful teaching tools for new students. I tell them not to think that the birds are lovely and peaceful while the trucks and helicopters disturb their zazen. "Rather," I say, "hear the birds singing as birds, the trucks singing as trucks, the helicopters singing as helicopters." There is a certain quiet and stillness behind and through all the sound and noise. Perfect quiet is not present until the heart is quiet

That said, it is good to sit in a quiet room, as Dōgen advises—especially for new practitioners. While there is ultimately no difference between silence and noise, between stillness and motion, between peace and disturbance, sitting in a still and quiet place may help us to better realize this.

Next, Dōgen explains the mental attitude of zazen, which, as we've seen, is to not judge or get mentally involved with ideas, people, events, or our surroundings.

> Put aside all involvements, give all affairs a rest. Think of neither good nor bad, right nor wrong. Stop the whirling wheels of mind, will, and consciousness, cease the measures and judgments of your inner thoughts, ideas, and impressions.

This is so important. We are constantly judging things and thinking about people and events, real and imagined. We think about what happened yesterday with joy or regret, we worry about what might happen tomorrow, we plan our busy todays. We judge the people in our lives as friends or enemies, and we judge events as acceptable or unacceptable. Zazen gives us a break from all that.

When sitting, stop judging things and just let them be as they are. We have opinions about so many things, even rainy days and sunny days. If you are a farmer, you might welcome a rainy day to water your fields, but if you are planning a picnic, then a rainy day might ruin your plans. When sitting zazen we keep a different attitude: "Rain is just rain, sun is just sun." Each is just what it is. We view each with equanimity, and we welcome each in its own time, putting aside judgments of good or bad.

All of life is made up of sunny days and rainy days. We like to be healthy but we don't like to be sick. We like to be young and dislike getting old. We welcome happy times such as the birth of a child, and we cry at sad times when a loved one dies. We like when things go our way, we resist or dislike when they don't. Śākyamuni Buddha called this *duḥkha* or "suffering." When we want X, but life gives us Y, the gap arising out of our disappointment creates mental resistance and upset. This is duḥkha. Our zazen practice closes that gap.

When sitting zazen, sick days are just sick days, healthy days are just healthy days. When young, just be young, and when grown old, just be old. When there is birth, let there be birth, and at the time of death, let death be. All is just as it is. This is the equanimity of Buddha.

However, we also learn that we don't have to be equanimous all the time. Or rather, we learn to feel equanimity and no equanimity at once, as if we were experiencing the same events in two different ways simultaneously. This is a fantastic power. If we only had equanimity, then humankind would be in a terrible condition. We would let tigers eat us instead of running away, and we would complacently walk off cliffs. We would never have discovered fire because we would have been content to stay in our caves and die of cold or hunger. Some days we would not even bother to get out of bed in the morning.

I do not want to be so unmoved, so equanimous, that I feel nothing when my mother dies or my child gets sick, On the other hand, it is our modern disease to rarely be content, and we have forgotten how to accept life on its own terms. That is not good either. We constantly resist life, regret yesterday, worry about tomorrow, and feel disappointment today when something does not measure up to our desires.

So is there a way to be both moved and unmoving at once? Yes! That way is zazen.

Let me tell you a story. A friend of mine—a long-time Zen practitioner—developed terminal cancer. It was very hard for her and for her family, which included young children. However, because she developed great wisdom from her Zen practice, she shared with me how she was able to feel many things at once. First, she resisted and fought the good fight for a cure through her radiation and chemotherapy, but at the same time she completely dropped all resistance, even welcomed this difficulty in her life. She described it as "resistance without resistance." It was as if she was seeing life one way with one eye and another way with her other eye. Having both eyes open brought clarity and wisdom to the situation.

She did sometimes feel overwhelming sadness and grief when she thought of her family, and especially her children, as any mother would. Nonetheless, she also found great peace within and a subtle sense that all was as it must be, that all would be fine. When we find this place of non-resistance, we are "trusting the universe to do its thing." It may not be the thing we personally want in that moment, but we develop an attitude that says, "Well, the universe brought me this far, handed me this body and this situation and this family. Thank you. And since it got me this far, it might as well just keep going where it goes, and I will go along for the ride."

At the height of her cancer, my friend profoundly realized this acceptance and let us share it with her. She would be leaving her beloved family, yet, in another way, she would never leave, for there had never been any possibility of standing even slightly apart from anyone or anything. When she experienced her cancer and sorrow, she also experienced a deep sense that she was the great moving cycle of this world, and that all her loved ones were too. In that way, she would never truly go anywhere when she died, because the world would keep turning, the flowers blooming, the wind blowing. She felt great peace, great wholeness, great trust that this life is not only what meets the eye, and death is not just an ending. Experiencing this brought her not only comfort, but also a profound realization about who we are. Knowing that we are all things and they are us also brought peace to her family and friends after she was gone.

Zazen is a means to let us see life in these two ways. We are fragile individuals, but also the whole that can never be broken.

> Give up even the aim of becoming a Buddha. This is true [not only for zazen but for all your daily actions] whether moving, standing, sitting, or lying down.

A living, breathing Buddha is someone who knows the peace and fullness that comes from the freedom from seeking, from the need to fill a sense of lack. The best means to be Buddha is to give up the need to do anything besides sitting (or walking when walking, standing when standing, lying in a sickbed when so lying), including giving up the need to become Buddha.

Zazen is thus a counterintuitive approach to achievement through the dropping away of the need to achieve. This is why shikantaza zazen is said to not be meditation. Shikantaza is a way of achieving something that can only come from setting aside for a time our human hungers, goals, and dissatisfactions. Yet, from the other side, we could misunderstand this goalless practice. We sit zazen as the one act that we need to do, the only place we need to be. But we can't keep sitting forever. We have to eventually get up from the cushion and live the rest of our life.

However, there is a big difference before and after zazen. After sitting, we also come to experience life two ways at once, as if seeing out of two eyes which together bring clarity. When we get up from the cushion, hopefully we bring that sense of fulfillment, peace, and acceptance with us—even as we set out to fix what needs to be fixed.

This is why Dōgen said that radical goallessness is true not only for zazen but for all our daily actions

One of my students is a medical worker in Africa. He administers vaccinations and basic medical care, battling each day to treat sick people and counter the effects of hunger and poverty. It seems like a never-ending struggle, and each day contains both victories and defeats. However, my student has told me several times that he would likely have burned out long ago and given up in frustration and disappointment if it was not for the power that zazen and his Zen practice give him. He cures diseases of the body, but his own dis-ease is treated each day by the power of zazen. We call his practice "struggling without struggling" and "acceptance without acceptance." The peace and equanimity that he has realized in zazen has in no way kept him from helping people and pushing for changes in economic and social policies. Instead, it has fueled his desire to strive for change.

## The Mechanics of Sitting

Let us look a bit more at the mechanics of zazen. Dōgen says:

At the place where we sit we usually spread a thick mat, on top of which we use a round cushion. Sit either in the full lotus posture or in the half lotus posture. For the full lotus posture, first put the right foot on the left thigh, then put the left foot on the right thigh. For the half lotus posture, just place the left foot onto the right thigh. Let your clothing hang loosely and make it neat. Then place the right hand over the left foot, and place the left hand on the right palm. The thumb-tips should lightly touch.

Just sit upright, not leaning to the left, inclining to the right, slouching forward, or arching backward. It is vital that the ears are on a plane with the shoulders, and the nose is in line with the navel. Let the tongue rest against the roof of the mouth. The lips and teeth are closed. The

eyes should be kept open. Let the breath pass impercepti-
bly through the nose. Having readied the posture, make
one full exhalation, and sway left and right. Then, sit
upright in balance, stable and solid.

We sit as still and upright as a mountain. The lotus postures that
Dōgen describes are stable and balanced postures that are intended to
let us forget about the body, because the stability and balance of the
body facilitates the stability and balance of the mind. In effect, these
two are so integrated that we describe them as "not two," or simply as
"bodymind." That said, many people cannot easily sit in the cross-
legged postures. For that reason, most contemporary teachers in the
West recommend students try other seating methods such as kneeling
on a *seiza* bench or sitting in a chair, so long as they are able to achieve
stability, balance, and comfort in these positions. Students should
each know their own bodies and needs. Even during a single sitting,
the body may naturally change, requiring small adjustments in posture from time to time. The point is to place the body in a stable, balanced seated position, and then stop thinking about it.

An important exception is for students who cannot sit comfortably
because of health issues such as chronic pain. To them I advise that
they take the most comfortable posture they can find, even if their
"sitting" is not sitting at all. I have one student with a bad back who
reclines on his side, and another who must stand. Even so, they tell me
that they still experience pain. For them, I must emphasize the attitude of accepting rain as rain. Since they have little choice, they have
to be with the pain, letting it be pain without judgment. It is not easy,
but they can learn the lesson that feeling pain and obsessing about it
are two different things. Zazen may not be able to assist much with
the former, but it can do wonders about the latter.

Students who struggle with pain can also try other techniques, like
following the breath, pouring themselves into breathing, or even reciting a mantra (a word or short phrase, chosen for meaning or just sound,
repeated in the mind for its focusing and mesmerizing quality) or

humming silently to distract themselves from the painful sensations. These aids may be necessary and helpful sometimes, as may be medication prescribed by doctors. But whenever possible, they should also learn to not run from the pain, letting the pain be the pain without adding sorrow or resistance. This is the lesson of shikantaza: accepting, even welcoming, one's lot, especially when one cannot change it.

Continuing with the posture, we put our hands in the zazen mudra pose by resting one hand on the other and bringing the thumbs together. Doing so contributes to our balance and stability, but the roundness of the mudra also stands for the roundness and openness of our mind. We place the tongue against the roof of the mouth because it suppresses the need for constant swallowing. Even if sitting in a chair or on a bench, we try to keep the back upright but not stiff. We don't slouch or lean sideways. Again, we need to have a sense of our own bodies, and look for a posture that feels supportive, stable, and comfortable.

Then, I encourage those who have difficulty allowing the mind to relax and settle, especially beginners, to place their attention on the breath, simply feeling it enter and exit the body through the nose. There is no need to follow it with the words "In, Out." Instead, the instruction is to just feel it.

On days in which your head is particularly filled with thoughts and emotions and you feel that you cannot settle down at all, you can count the breaths instead of merely following, moving from one to ten at the top of each breath. But don't try to do anything unusual, such as forcing or lengthening the breath. Just let it take its natural pattern—breathe short breaths as short and long breaths as long. That said, it is advisable to breathe deeply from the diaphragm by letting the stomach move in and out with each breath, imagining that the inhalation and exhalation originates below the navel.

For more advanced practitioners who already know how to settle the mind, I recommend that they sit focused in open, spacious awareness rather than on the breath. The focus of attention in open, spacious awareness is then everything. It is rather like the attitude drivers have when driving down the highway—they are attentive to the road as a whole, but do not think about anything specifically. This attitude of alertness and attention is important. Although we are not thinking about anything specific, we should avoid being listless, sitting like a bump on a log during our zazen. We just need to relax, and be alert and attentive to the zazen road.

In Dōgen's shikantaza, we generally face the wall. Our eyes are about one-third open, looking at either the wall or, if there is no wall, the floor. The reason that we do not fully close our eyes is to embody an attitude in which we are neither escaping from the world nor running toward it. For example, the table across the room may be somewhere in our field of vision, but we do not think about it; we do not even label it as "table," or think "there is a table over there." It is just in our field of vision. Certainly, we don't want to get caught in long streams of thoughts, such as, "Oh, there is that table—that ugly table. I need to buy a new table today. I wonder if there are any new ones on sale at the shops . . ." If we see spots on the wall, we just see them. We avoid being caught up in thinking about them: "Gee, those spots joined together look just like Abraham Lincoln," or, "What a dirty wall; I need to clean it." It may be good to clean the wall, but please wait to do so until after zazen is finished. During zazen we just sit zazen.

If you do find yourself caught in streams of thought, return to following the breath or to open, spacious awareness. Repeat as needed, gently returning each time. Let the thought train continue down the tracks without your stoking the engine or remaining on board, and return to just sitting.

This brings us to the vital matter of the mind during zazen. Dōgen now says:

Think of not thinking. How do you think of not thinking? Non-thinking. This itself is the essential art of zazen.

This instruction is, perhaps, the very heart of "Fukan Zazengi."

Note the distinction Dōgen makes between thinking, not thinking, and the state that transcends both—non-thinking. Other translators have rendered the question above as, "How can the state beyond thinking be thought about? It is different from thinking," and, "How do you think of not thinking? Beyond-thinking."

It sounds mysterious. Let me offer my interpretation.

Human beings engage in thought from morning until night. We analyze, plan, categorize, and judge. We divide the world into mental images, some of which we love, some of which we don't. This is thinking.

During zazen, thoughts continue to come and go, but we do not engage them. By not engaging them, we encounter space between and behind the thoughts where the analysis, categorization, division, and judgment stops. As I have mentioned, many traditional commentators have compared this state of mind to a clear, open, boundless sky. There is a sense of clarity, a lack of friction, a feeling of peace in our minds. This is not thinking.

Beyond that, as the thoughts and emotions drift through the mind like clouds migrating through the open sky, the clarity and light of the sky illuminate those same thoughts. They become lighter, translucent. Problems become less problematic, life's complexity is simplified. Thoughts and problematic situations may remain, yet somehow are not as before. This is non-thinking, sometimes called thinking-not-thinking—the very essence of zazen. So, the simplicity of zazen is, at the same time, a total release and freedom without bounds. In this state, we are truly at home.

> Zazen is not step-by-step mastering meditative concentration. It is simply the the peaceful and joyful gate of the Buddha's truth, the practice and realization of the Buddha's complete enlightenment. It is the kōan right here realized; nothing can catch or ensnare it. The truth appears, there being no delusion. If you understand this, you are like a dragon that has reached the waters or a tiger reposing on

its mountain. The right order of things will then be apparent, and all darkness and confusion will drop away from the start.

Dōgen emphasizes that shikantaza is not step-by-step meditation whose purpose is to reach various levels of practice or concentration. It is just the "peaceful and joyful gate of the Buddha's truth," the practice that embodies the Buddha's complete enlightenment itself. He then employs the powerful image of two great creatures completely at home in their elements—the dragon in its watery lair and the tiger atop the mountain—to convey the powerful feeling of belonging that arises in zazen.

But we cannot remain seated on our cushion. At the end of seated zazen, we must get back to life, to do all the things we need to do, to live with our thoughts and emotions. But much of that peace and ease, that sense of freedom and release, will remain in our hearts. We take with us the insight we've gleaned from non-thinking as we return to our thinking and busy lives.

When you arise from sitting, move slowly and stand up calmly. Do not rise hurriedly or abruptly.

At the completion of zazen, as we rise from sitting, we move our body slowly and stand up calmly, without violence and hurry. We then encounter our ordinary, tedious, and frequently troubling world and daily life as extraordinary.

By virtue of zazen, many have transcended the common and the sacred. Some died while sitting, while others died standing, relying fully on this power of zazen.

The wisdom derived from zazen is so profound that Zen masters of the past were even able to see beyond, not only ordinary and sacred, but also life and death, to a vision that transcends coming and going, birth and death. Many chose to die in the lotus posture, others while standing—all relying on the power of zazen.

> Moreover, our discriminating mind can never understand how the Buddhas and Ancestors manifested the essence of Zen with finger, pole, needle, or mallet, or how they passed on realization with a hossu, fist, staff, or shout. Nor can this be grasped through supernatural powers or a dualistic view of practice and enlightenment. Zazen is a practice beyond sound and form and all the subjective and objective worlds, a practice preceding all discriminating thinking and perceptions.

Dōgen never advocates or gives instruction for focusing on a kōan during zazen. However, he himself did cherish kōans as teaching parables, and as themes to riff on in his *Shōbōgenzō* and elsewhere. He sometimes suggested that a student chew on a famous kōan at a time other than zazen. He emphasized that the act of zazen is, in fact, the embodiment of the wisdom that is the central point of many kōans. He felt that the act of sitting is itself a realized kōan.

In "Fukan Zazengi," Dōgen compares zazen to several kōans, each expressing the coming together of this divided world and the undivided realm of Buddha. For example, in one famous kōan, Master Jùzhī (Gutei in Japanese), whenever he was asked about Zen, would simply hold up one finger. In another, Mahākāśyapa asked Ānanda, the Buddha's attendant and cousin, to take down the flagpole that was raised at the monastery at times of debate, signaling that the time for discourse or reflection was over. Nāgārjuna wished to demonstrate the relationship of individual things to unbroken wholeness by dropping a thin needle into a bowl of water where it vanished from sight—present yet invisible. And the bodhisattva Mañjuśrī banged his gavel to signal the start of a talk by the Buddha, a talk in which the teacher spoke no words.

One day, the Buddha ascended to his teaching seat. Mañjuśrī struck the table with a mallet and said, "When one realizes the Dharma King's Dharma teachings, the Dharma teachings of the Dharma King are just thus!" Thereupon the Buddha descended from the teaching seat. (*Book of Serenity*, Case 1.)

To embody and express the power and wholeness beyond words, some Zen teachers would draw circles in the air with their *hossu*, a traditional whisk used by an abbot, or make a fist (the separate fingers coming together as one), strike the ground with their staff to show "just this," or give a shout. For Dōgen, the act of sitting zazen is likewise the very embodiment and expression of the finger, the fist, a strike, a shout. Zazen is where the wordless wholeness of this unity and this separation are one beyond one, "just this," and the needle vanishes in the waters.

When we drop the discriminating mind in zazen, the meaning of these kōans and strange actions can become clear. As Dōgen notes, this is not an understanding that needs some supernatural, otherworldly, or psychic powers to attain, nor is this an understanding possible through a dualistic view that we practice in order to attain some knowledge separate from here. Dōgen indicates again that zazen is not a dualistic practice to attain enlightenment, but is the practice of enlightenment itself.

In some of his other writings, Dōgen also spoke of the true power of zazen to make whole this broken world as a power much more fantastic than the kinds of mystical or supernatural powers that people sometimes seek in their spiritual practices, both in Dōgen's day and today. In other writings, he made the point that the true "wondrous powers" of the Zen master are such ordinary acts as sipping tea, sleeping when tired, cutting wood, and hauling water, doing daily work for the community, or simply being kind to others. The miracle of our aliveness and our ability to do these so-called "ordinary" things is truly extraordinary.

Therefore, no distinction should be made between the
smart and the dull. It is not a matter of intelligence or education. To practice single-heartedly is, in itself, negotiating
the Way and attaining the truth. Practice and enlightenment are untainted, and are an everyday affair.

He also repeatedly emphasized that this practice is open to anyone, and that we do not need to be particularly intelligent or have
special education in order to do zazen. When speaking to house-
holders, Dōgen would frequently emphasize that this practice was
open to people living in the world; though sometimes, when addressing monastics, Dōgen would emphasize monasticism as the
unique vehicle for practice. He knew his audience and the inspiration they needed! Here, in "Fukan Zazengi," he is writing advice to
one of his lay followers living out in the world, so we can be assured
that Dōgen meant this for all of us. In fact, zazen transcends monastery walls, town or country. A moment of zazen is the whole world
in all directions.

The Buddhas and Ancestors, in India and in China, in this
world and in any world, have all preserved these customs
and traditions and maintain the Buddha's authentic seal.
Thus, we must devote ourselves exclusively to and be completely absorbed in the practice of zazen, total commitment
to just sitting. Although it is said that there are countless
distinctions and innumerable ways of understanding Buddhism, we should pursue the Way by undertaking zazen
alone.

Here is where Dōgen again turns to the core of shikantaza. When
sitting zazen, we must sit as a sacred and flawless act, as if all the Buddhas and Ancestors were sitting as our sitting. The sitter should trust in
their bones that the mere act of sitting is Buddha come to life on the
sitting cushion. To experience the state of Buddha, we must sit in the

wholeness and completion of Buddha. When we sit, we might feel that the whole universe is present on our *zafu*, therefore we sit at the heart of life. This may sound romantic, but we should sit with this attitude.

> There is no reason to leave your own sitting place and make aimless trips to dusty foreign lands. When your first step is mistaken, you will stumble right past the great way that is immediately before you.

People think that if they travel far, to Japan or Tibet, to a temple on some holy mountain, they will find true Buddhism. Unfortunately, they are like dogs chasing their own tails; they do not realize that what they need has been here all along. Dōgen himself once traveled to China in search, only to realize that what he had been seeking had been everywhere all along:

> You have had the extreme good fortune to be born with a human body, so do not pass this time in vain.

Some people think that because zazen is described as goalless or beyond right and wrong, that it does not matter how it is done. This is not true. We must diligently and sincerely practice this goallessness by sitting in a balanced posture and dropping all thoughts of right and wrong. It is a conundrum, but as we go to our cushions, we must be diligent and sit in the place of "no place to go." We must devote some time to this each day, yet once sitting, drop all measures of time.

We sit each day for a certain amount of time—ten to thirty minutes or so—but we do so with a profound conviction that zazen is not a matter of long or short, and that even an instant of zazen holds all the time of the universe. Although we sit with the realization that time can't ultimately ever be wasted, we had best not waste it on measuring time. We sit zazen trusting that it is beyond measure and that this very act is already the fulfillment of all time and achievement. And though time is beyond measure, and every moment is precious in itself and cannot be wasted, it would also be a waste of this lifetime if we fail to sit zazen and diligently practice in order to embody such fact.

> Now that you know what is the most important essence of the Buddha's truth, how can you be satisfied merely with this capricious world as transient as sparks from a flint? Our bodies are like dew on a blade of grass, and our lives pass like a flash of lightning, vanishing in an instant.

This life may be precious, but if we become too attached to its shiny baubles, to petty matters, and our small human struggles, we might miss addressing the big questions, the truly important matters of who we are in this universe, and how best to live in it during our short lives. Do not miss this chance to face what is vital.

> Earnest followers of Zen, do not be overwhelmed by the real dragon or stop for only part of an elephant. Devote yourself to the way which points directly to suchness. Honor those who are beyond attainment and intention, with nothing more to do. Accord with the wisdom of the Buddhas and become a rightful successor to the enlightenment of the Ancestors. If you sit zazen in such a way for a time, you will realize such completely. The treasure-house will then open of itself, and you will be able to receive and employ its contents to your heart's content.

Do not be distracted by cheap imitations and partial truths, Dōgen says. He then refers to a story about a man who collected toy dragons, but had no idea what a real dragon was, even when it was right before his eyes. He also quotes the famous story of six blind men touching bits of an elephant, unable to fathom the whole for the pieces. One of the men, having touched the elephant's head, thought an elephant was like a jar. The second, touching its ear, said it was like a basket. The third likened the trunk to a snake. The fourth thought the elephant's side was a wall. The fifth that the leg was like a tree trunk. And the sixth equated the tail with a rope. These people could not recognize the real and the whole.

Please sit zazen and embody the real and the whole.

Zazen is a most unusual practice in which we radically abandon all search for treasure in order to realize the treasure that was our birthright all along. How strange to give up searching for something that we think is missing, thereby to know the completeness of what is already present. When we think something is lacking and believe it is only to be found far away, we render it distant. But when we give up all feelings of gain and loss, all is fulfilled. When we drop all ideas of near and far, the distant is found to be close at hand.

Dōgen said that zazen is for everyone. But we must not forget the other meaning of this: When we sit, we do not sit just for ourselves. We sit for all suffering sentient beings everywhere. One for all and all as one. Dōgen hoped that everyone would join him in sitting this way, thus he called his piece "Fukan Zazengi" (The Way of Zazen Recommended for Everyone).

Dōgen's recommendations give us a wise way to face life's trials.

# Realizing the Truth Right Here

## GENJŌ KŌAN

Perhaps the clearest and most concise description of Dōgen's great dance—the dance of enlightenment—is in a letter he wrote to one of his many lay students. We only know that Japanese student's name and the place where he lived. He was Koshu Yō of Kyushu Island. Koshu Yō, like countless Zen seekers before and after him, seems to have been looking for guidance about his Zen practice in order to know himself and his place in this world. Dōgen showed him—as he shows us—how to look through the problems and complexities of this world, and practice and know enlightenment right here. That is one way to read the title "Genjō Kōan" (Realizing the Truth Right Here). Dōgen is teaching us to encounter this life from several perspectives at once (and from the perspective of no perspective, where there is no separation between the seer and the seen).

To summarize Dōgen's perspectives, they are ways to see, know, and embody unity and wholeness in this often rough, sometimes disappointing world. One way to accomplish this is to become free of the many judgments, demands, hungers, frictions, frustrations, and fears of our apparently separate self when it views itself as distinct from, and in frequent conflict with, the world "outside" it. There is something more—something beyond that separation and conflict. Our moment-by-moment practice is the key to realizing so. This is the core message of the "Genjō Kōan."

To know and experience the world from these vantage points helps liberate us from suffering. That may not seem like practical advice for dealing with the reality of our daily troubles, but it is the most practical advice on how to be free in this life—to discover who we truly are.

Because Dōgen's words can be a bit hard to fathom sometimes, rather than work with a strict translation, in some portions of the following text I am going to play with and expand on Dōgen's words to make his points shine through. I hope he would forgive me. If readers would like to see what I have added or how I have altered the original, please compare my words to any of the fine translations available. I think you will see that I maintain the heart of Dōgen's words, while hopefully making them a bit more accessible.

Dōgen begins by offering a first perspective on the world in which ordinary beings come and go between birth and death. In contrast, Buddhas, which embody idealized perfection, seem to stand above us, different and far distant:

> When things are seen as separate in the Buddha's teach-
> ings, there is human delusion, there is distant enlighten-
> ment, and there is Buddhist practice to move us from the
> former to the latter, there is birth and there is death, and
> there are Buddhas and sentient beings that stand apart.

That is the view we hold, especially when first starting on the Buddhist path, when the world seems mostly divided. We desire to climb from our present fallen state to the height of perfection and the freedom of a Buddha.

But Master Dōgen then points us to another way of experiencing truth:

When the myriad things are realized as each without an
individual self, there is no delusion and no enlightenment,
no Buddhas and no sentient beings, no birth and no death.

This is the truth of "emptiness," in which categories and names for
separate things are swept into wholeness. We can encounter the world
this other way too, without making judgments of near or far, flawed or
flawless, perfect or imperfect, high or low, and without applying mental categories and thoughts of separation. Then the division of ordinary beings and Buddhas evaporates, and the strife of this world vanishes too. Buddhas and sentient beings are then experienced as not
apart, not separate. Enlightenment is never hidden—even in the
world of confusion—once we learn to see. We can drop away our ideas
of coming and going, birth and death, and instead experience an ongoing continuity and wholeness beyond time, beyond birth and death.
    Yet we must not stop there, for we must keep living in this world
that is also separate things, coming and going:

    In the Buddha Way, we must leap clear of and right through
    both the view of fullness and the view of lack; thus there
    are again birth and death, delusion and enlightenment,
    sentient beings and Buddhas.

We can experience this life and world in both of the foregoing ways
at once. The result is a bit tricky to get one's head around, but it is
based on wisdom. We learn to see through all the divisions and seeming imperfections of the world, even as they appear to continue to
exist. For example, we see many flaws in life and society, yet we also
learn to drop all judgments about what is flawed or flawless. Instead,
all things become just what they are without our criticism, each a
shining jewel in its own way, even those things that we usually resist
or find abhorrent.
    However, that does not mean that we simply tolerate those flaws
either: the uglier and more abhorrent something is, the more deeply

buried and hard to see is that shining light. Thus, although this world and all things may shine from within (and so, from that perspective, they do so without need of polishing to remove the grime which obscures), we still have to keep polishing in our practice to bring out that shine. Although Buddhas and ordinary sentient beings are not apart, if ordinary beings continue to think and act ignorantly, they will not realize this truth. We have to think (and nonthink, putting aside divisive and judgmental thoughts) and act more like Buddhas would act, freeing ourselves from excess desires, anger, and divided thinking in order to make the presence of Buddha appear before our eyes and in our hearts. This is Dōgen's path of "practice-enlightenment," in which we practice acting as a Buddha now in order to realize that Buddha has been here all along. Even when we don't think and act like it, the fact is that we are still Buddha nonetheless, although our ignorance and poor behavior will keep that truth hidden from us and cause suffering.

Yet, even with all our insight and wisdom, even when realizing this hard world as shining Buddha, this world remains hard nonetheless. So, Dōgen writes:

> Yet even so, the beloved flowers still fall to our regret and sorrow, the weeds still grow though we wish it were not so.

Delusion and enlightenment, ordinary sentient beings and Buddhas, are apart yet not apart from one another; the same, yet not at all as they were before realization. But even with such wisdom and insight, even while seeing something beyond the flaws of this sometimes very hard world, we remain human, fragile, sometimes heartbroken.

This world may have aspects of a dream, but it can often be a very hard dream. For example, I may tell someone who has experienced the loss of a loved one that death is not all that meets the eye when we realize a timeless reality which flows on and on. Still, that does not keep their heart from aching. I cannot tell soldiers and hungry children that violence and injustice are caused by the delusions of anger and desire, and that they should simply see through it all to a vision in which there is nothing to fight for and nothing lacking. Although there is such an insight to experience, doing so does not end the very real bloodshed and hunger. We still have to work to end the war and feed the children.

This world will still break our hearts sometimes, even if we see through the curtain of delusion. Dōgen taught us to see through loss and separation into a realm in which nothing can ever be lost or apart. Nonetheless, as he notes, the flowers we love will sometimes still fall, the weeds we resist will still grow.

In his wisdom, Dōgen remained the warm human being and poet of joy and sadness who felt that we should not—must not—turn ourselves into ice and stone, removed from all human emotion and pain. He once wrote, for example, of his own tears on the death anniversary of his beloved teacher, Rujing:

> Today I offer incense for my late teacher, an ancient Buddha.... Five thousand miles of ocean are filled with my sorrowful tears; for twenty years now, so much heartbreak![2]

Despite having the key to see through all human loss and suffering, even birth and death, he was still content to know ordinary human pathos. His poetry shows he was such a man, such as in the image of flowers falling.

No matter how wise and insightful any of us may become, the world remains a hard place. That's okay, Dōgen assures us. We can feel sorrow when we lose our loved ones. We can cry for all the children who are suffering in this world.

This is where our work comes in. We might say that our task as human beings is to live in this sometimes hard and painful world, yet to also see through it—to not become prisoners of our pain, fears, and sense of lack. At the same time, we must constantly work to make this world better where we can, even if many flaws and evils remain.

And so, Dōgen next addresses these questions: How are we to be free of our suffering and the ignorance that is our usual way of viewing this world, even as we still live in this sometimes sorrowful and disappointing world? How can we attain true insight to see beyond surface appearances? What is the cause of our ignorance? He writes:

> It is delusion to impose yourself and your desires upon life, demanding that the myriad things of the world be as you wish.

According to Dōgen and countless other Buddhist teachers, we mistakenly try to bend the world to our desires so it will live up to our demands, dreams, and wishes.

Isn't this what we try to do, sometimes successfully but often not—to get life to bend to and fit our demands? Is that the only way to live? Goals and dreams help us achieve great and small things and they are necessary to living, but is there also a way to know life without demands and expectations? Zazen shows us that we can encounter this life and world as they are, on their own terms, without imposing our self and its selfish demands upon them.

> To let the myriad things be as they are, illuminating yourself, is enlightenment.

But, in fact, counsels Dōgen, it is possible to both have our dreams and wishes and also be free of them, the "best of both worlds" that are just this one world all along:

> Buddhas are those with great understanding of the nature of delusion. Alas, confused beings are those who are greatly deluded about the nature of enlightenment. Moreover, because life is not stagnant, so a Buddha must continue to realize realization upon realization, while ordinary folks just fall into delusion after delusion.

Practitioners sometimes think that enlightenment is the endpoint of practice rather than an ongoing series of daily actions that are each an opportunity to manifest either ignorant or enlightened behavior. They think that they must get to a perpetually blissful place called "enlightenment," removed from the pain and complexity of this world, and all their problems will disappear but their wishes and desires will be fully satisfied. Actually, that has never been the way Zen masters considered enlightenment, or, at least, a complete vision of it. While there is a state beyond self and problems—a place where all desires are satisfied in unbroken wholeness—human beings cannot live there. They cannot pay the bills and fall in love there. So, we should realize that instead we can experience a flawed world that is also flawless. We can have goals and expectations and demands, yet also accept life as it is, on its own terms. In other words, we can know a realm of endless peace, beyond all lack and ugliness, as one with this world of frequent disturbance, lack, and ugliness.

I know this might sound a bit ethereal and impractical. We turn on the news, or just look around in our own families or neighborhoods, and we see so much that is difficult about the world. Maybe we feel hopeless, without the peace and strength to keep going. However, we do not realize that we can both accept suffering and work to alleviate it. We Zen practitioners take what we call "bodhisattva vows," in which we dedicate ourselves to the rescue of all sentient beings: but we do so knowing that such beings are numberless and suffering never ends. Yet, from another angle, we also see that there have never been separate beings in need of rescue, nor anything lacking from the start. Manifesting our buddha nature, our inner Buddha-like qualities of wisdom and compassion, means to not stand frozen and outside life, but rather to see through our greed, anger, and ignorance, even as we learn to live free of them. In other words, we can work to make this world better, all while knowing that such work can never fully succeed because this complicated world will always be somehow flawed (all while knowing, from yet another angle, that there was never flaw or lack from the start!). Manifesting our wisdom and compassion, we can know the world all these ways at once!

Some mystics say, "In the world, yet not fully of the world." Wisdom is sometimes compared to the beautiful lotus flower that rises from the mud, that takes the mud and muck and turns it into its own beauty. So even though the lotus is rooted in the ugly mud, it is not bound by the sordid, it is nurtured by the mud, and produces something lovely amid the ugliness. Dōgen goes on:

> Buddha doesn't need to note she is Buddha. Nevertheless, Buddhas are just living Buddhas who keep on living Buddha by bringing Buddha to life.

When you manifest Buddha, you do so in each wise and compassionate thought, word, and deed, great or small, of your daily life. Buddha's action is not a fancy gesture you need to stick a flag on, make a big show about, or hire a marching band to proclaim. Buddha is wondrous, yet quite ordinary. I personally see Buddha manifesting all around me, not with a golden body and a shining halo floating high in the sky, but in the simple acts of generosity, peace, love, kindness, and harmony carried out by ordinary people in this world each day. Whenever a human being acts with generosity and altruism rather than selfishness, when she offers peace where there was strife or sees though division to the unity of all things, then she is bringing Buddha to life in this world and time. The person so acting need not even note to herself that she is doing so.

> When one sees the forms or hears the sounds of the world fully and wholly with body and mind [free of judgment, free of mental categories, transcending "me, my, mine"], one intimately understands without separation. Then, it is not like some object and its reflection in a mirror, and it is unlike the moon and its reflection in distant water, whereby one side is illuminated and the other side is left in the dark.

Most of us feel cut off from life much of the time, as if our self and the rest of the world were separate. Frictions and disappointments come out of this sense of separation. But there is a way to experience life so unified, so intimate, that such frictions and disappointments drop away. It takes a sense of separation to have tumult and trouble. So, let's just stop feeling that separation! Give up sticking so stubbornly to this sense of our separate selves via our Buddhist practice. Then, one sees both sides at once, wholeness and separation, completion and lack, as two sides of a single no-sided coin, and all is illuminated.

For to master the Buddha Way is to learn the self. To learn the self is to drop the separate self from mind. To drop the separate self from mind is to be actualized by the myriad things of the world. When actualized by the myriad things, one's body and mind as well as the bodies and minds of others all drop away. In such intimacy, no trace even of "enlightenment" remains, and this no-trace continues endlessly.

The self is filled with all manner of drives and desires, as well as feelings of isolation from everything and everyone that is not itself. You are frustrated when the world fails to meet your terms and conditions. Please study that, then stop that! Then all the world comes to embrace you without terms and conditions, unifying all life. This "life-self-world" becomes so fluid, whole, and natural that there is no need to label it even with a term like "enlightenment."

When you first seek the Buddha's truth, you imagine you are far away from its locale. However, Buddha's truth is already correctly transmitted right here; realizing so, you are immediately your original self.

When you sail in a boat and look out at the shore, you might feel that the shore is moving. But when you turn your eyes toward the boat, you may then feel that the boat is moving. In the same way, if you observe the myriad things of the world with confused ideas of body and mind you might assume that your mind and nature are enduring and stand separate from things. But when you intimately practice and turn within, it will become clear that nothing at all has a fixed, individual self.

Until this moment, maybe you thought that you were a single, independent, sometimes lonely, isolated, frustrated being living apart from the rest of life. Maybe you felt like a lone sailor struggling on a boat, fighting the wind and ocean currents, with the shore moving swiftly by. But in zazen, that separation melts in such a way that sailor and sea and shore and sail and wind, and the other sailors and vessels and lands to the horizon and beyond, prove to be a single whole, and all flow as the true nature of the sea that was our nature all along.

Firewood turns to ash and it does not turn to firewood again. But do not think that the ash is the future and the firewood is past. Rather, ash is wholly ash with nothing remaining, and the firewood is just firewood with nothing more. You should understand that firewood abides in the phenomenal expression and wholeness of firewood, which fully includes its own past and future yet is independent of all past and future. Ash abides in the phenomenal expression and wholeness of ash, which fully includes its own past and future too.

We come to experience each moment of life as wholly what it is—a fully contained and actualized instant without comparison to any other moments of life. Of course, we live in a world of time, of before and after, past, present, and future. But we can come to see each instant as just that instant, its own fully contained moment of time that stands as its own shining jewel.

In the wintertime, we might make a fire that we think has a start, middle, and end. We think that the firewood burns away, leaving ash.

But is that the only way to experience fire? Can we also come to see each moment of burning as the only moment, and timeless? This same question applies to all the apparent changes of flowing time—including our lifetimes, which seem to burn away so quickly.

> Just as firewood does not turn to firewood again after it is ash, do not think of returning to birth after death.

What is true about fire is true about aging and death. Let us leave aside the mystery of what may or may not follow after death. Rather, let us just come to experience life wholly as the time of life, and when death comes, we experience it simply as the moment of death. Likewise, aging is just the time of aging, health the time of health, sickness the time of sickness.

> Thus, it is an established rule in Buddhist teachings to deny that birth turns into death. Therefore, birth is understood as no-birth, for in the time of birth there is no other moment with which to compare it. It is an unshakable teaching in Buddha's preaching that death does not turn into birth. Therefore, death is understood as no-death when there is no other moment with which to compare it.

When there is birth, there is only birth, and death is just the time of death. Life and death are each their own time and moment. When it is time for life, live gracefully, for your life depends on it. When it is time for death, please die thoroughly, right to the death! Both life and death are just this life. I believe that Dōgen is telling us to live fully this moment, to take this moment on its own terms and to live it well, making it the best moment that we can.

What is more, when we drop from our mind any ideas of opposites, such as start and finish, birth and death, might we know something that transcends and embraces them? It is like the steps and leaps of the dance. Before each step and after it, and as that one step itself, there is nothing but the dance flowing. The moon seems to rise in the evening and vanish at dawn, but in truth it is ever shining somewhere, and really has gone nowhere. There is something timeless, ever flowing and ever shining, at the heart of all the changes of time.

Not only can we experience each moment as all moments—much as we can perceive each moment of a single leap as embodying the whole dance of all leaps flowing on—but we can also experience each moment as the only moment beyond comparison. When a dancer leaps, leaping is just leaping; it is not descending. When the dancer descends and the leap ends, descending is just descending; it is not rising. Each step in each moment is the only step in that particular place and time. Each event of our lives is also the only moment in that place and time, so it is beyond comparison.

> Birth is a situation complete in this moment. Death is a situation complete in this moment. They are the same as winter and spring. We do not say that winter becomes spring, nor do we say that spring becomes summer.

All the seasons of life—birth, youth, aging, and dying—are just like this. Each is its own season, each is just the shining moon. So, winter is just winter, summer wholly summer, fall but fall, and spring is totally spring. In winter, live well and fully in winter, likewise in the other times. In each season, there is nothing else but this. So how is time even passing?

Everything happens in its own season. So it is for life and death.

> Our enlightenment is like the moon reflected in the water. The moon does not get wet, the water is not broken. Although the light shines wide and vast, the moon is reflected in a puddle a foot or an inch wide. The entire moon and the whole sky are reflected in countless dewdrops upon the grass, and even in a single drop of water.

This understanding comes when we learn to see and experience this world in all its variety and complexity, its division and separation, as variations and expressions of something wonderfully all-embracing, something beyond broken pieces and friction. Imagine that moon again, its light shining on and within all things. This moon represents the light of Buddha, what we call enlightenment.

This moonlight shines from within you too, *as* you. And you don't even need to do anything to make it so.

> Enlightenment does not divide a person, just as the moon does not shatter the water. We cannot obstruct enlightenment, just as a drop of water does not obstruct the moon in the sky. The depth of each drop is the measure of the height of the moon. No matter how long or short the duration of each reflection, it expresses the largeness or smallness of the dewdrop, yet completely holds the boundlessness of the moonlight in the heavens.

Not only you, but all people, things, and events are the moonlight shining: long things shining as long, short things shining as short; happy events are the moon shining happily, sad times are but the moon illuminated in sadness. All are the one moon. Nonetheless, although this light is always shining, our practice is to uncover that light within.

> So, when the Buddhist truth does not truly fill your whole body and mind, you think the situation is already enough and that you can stop. But when the Buddhist truth fills your body and mind, you understand that there is always something more, so you keep moving onward.

Don't be one of those people who tastes a little peace and timelessness on the meditation cushion or elsewhere in life then gets puffed up with such achievement, or disappointed when it does not last forever.

Better is the person of true freedom who can know a deep, abiding peace, sometimes felt and sometimes hidden like the moon, right in this world of peace and conflict, light and darkness, rain or shine. Better to be the person aware of timelessness even as the clock keeps ticking, as years pass, as youth fades, and as we grow older. Enlightenment is not a frozen event in time, but a living truth that we keep practicing in order to manifest its light. Enlightenment is like a sailing trip that continues through all weather and features, not something halted in a shapeless sea:

> For example, if someone sails in a boat out to the middle of the ocean where no land is in sight and looks all around, the ocean looks circular and empty, and does not look to have other form. But the ocean is truly not round or square, and its features are varied beyond count. It is like a palace of endless rooms. It is like a jewel of countless facets. It only looks circular and empty as far as seen by the eye at that time. All things of the world are like this.

The graceful dance goes on, and it is not a matter of stopping suddenly, finished or frozen on a barren stage. Calling some round, lifeless realm as "nirvana," as if some featureless and final ending, would be like a sailor in the open sea, surrounded by nothing but water, the bare horizon a circle in all directions, thinking that such was the whole world, and that he could stop right there forever. It is a kind of stagnation or anchoring that halts the voyage, missing true arrival at the shores of wisdom found all around. Be wise and welcome all the complexity, diversity, and impurities of this world as that same purity in a different guise. Welcome all of this life as if each aspect was just one of various rooms in a mansion, shining pearls on a string, flowers in a garden, moments in a dance, as if it was the moon reflected in endless forms in myriad pools of water. That goes for the parts of life you love, and those you do not.

Though the earthly world and the world-beyond-conditions
have so many features, we can perceive and understand
only as far as our eye can reach through practice. In order
to grasp the real nature of countless things, you must know
that the oceans and land have infinite varied features
besides their appearance as round or square. Whole worlds
are found all around. It is so, not only looking out to the
periphery, but also directly under your feet and in every
drop of water.

Welcome all the diversity of this ailing and healthy, up and down
world. This is where Buddhas come alive, where enlightenment is put
into action, where the moon shines to let all scenes glow. Don't try to
understand it all, don't try to master or control it. Rather, begin with
your own practice, right where you sit and stand and walk and breathe.
All the complex shapes of life are simplicity in another form. All the
rough and sharp edges are roundness in another expression. One who
understands this is truly a master.

A fish swims in its ocean, and no matter how far it swims,
the waters are without end. A bird flies through its sky, and
no matter how far it flies, the sky is without end. At the
same time, the fish and the bird have never left their water or
their sky. When their need is large their use will be large.
When the need is small their use is thus small. Thereby, each
of them totally uses its full range in each moment, and each
of them wholly brings its realm to vibrant activity. Yet, if the
bird were to leave the air, it would die at once. If the fish
were to depart from the water, it would die at once. Thus we
can conclude that water is life and air is life. Bird is life and
fish is life. Also, life is the bird and life is the fish. In this
same way, practice-enlightenment is the expression of
bounded and boundless life right here and now.

What a picture Dōgen paints of the deep interconnection and identity of everything, including our lives! Here he describes how life is a field of opportunity, and how it is up to us to make something of it. Of course, we are not totally free to do and be what we want, no more than a fish can leave the water or a bird can fly without the air. Nonetheless, where and how the bird or fish travel within their given medium, and with what grace and energy, is largely up to them.

Thus, practice never stops because the features and variety of our lives never stop, so we practice right here where we are. In this place and setting, in this facet of the whole, our practice brings life to life. This is the sea in which we sail or swim, the stage upon which we dance, the sky where we fly. The dancer brings the dance to life by being the dance. We are the life of this earth, and like the fish in the water and birds in the sky who bring water and sky to life, all this world is our extension, not merely our location.

This is your place, your life right here, and you cannot be anywhere other than where you find yourself so long as you are alive. So please live this life well and experience this place wisely. The possibilities, if not quite endless, are greatly up to you. We human beings cannot change all the circumstances in which we find ourselves, but within our realms we have more power than we know to range freely. Please swim or fly your course with grace and skill.

> If a bird or a fish attempts to fully explore the reaches of its field without swimming or flying in it, this bird or this fish will never find its way or place. But when we find our place where we are here and now, practice occurs that actualizes the universe. When we find our way in this moment, practice occurs that actualizes the universe.

Life must come to life, be lived, in you, and your life is life living. How you live, how you practice right now within this limited yet unlimited world, is where it all comes to life. This is the pivot point where you dance and swim and fly. You are here; where else can you be but the place you are? You cannot go ahead but from right here, you cannot do but do right here, you cannot stay up or fall but from right here, you cannot fly gracefully or fly gracelessly in any sky but right here, you cannot act in peace or in anger except right here. For example, if you choose to raise a fist in anger or to turn the other cheek, to say sweet words or ugly words, to be filled with greed or to act with charity, the place and time of action is always now and here. Life is made real by how you live it, here and now. This is practice-enlightenment.

> In truth, the place and the way are neither large nor small, are not just the self nor others. The place and the way are neither things that have come from the past, nor are they only arising now.

Right here is the pivot point of our life and practice. The happy places and sad places, the birth places and death places, the high places and low places are each and all right here. Further, your place and actions may seem small and finite, but they are also the whole universe and all the other things in it acting boundlessly in each small step and gesture. It is big things and small things and things beyond measure. It is you and others and neither you nor others. It comes from the past and heads into the future, yet each instant is timeless and it's only right now.

I like to remind people that, when they smile or cry, it is the whole universe smiling and crying. So take care of what is before you. This is where practice begins and where enlightenment is made real and brought to life. Each small act that you do, if appreciated as sacred and complete, is thoroughly undertaken as the whole universe.

> Equally, in the practice-enlightenment of the Buddha Way, truly meeting one thing is realizing one thing thoroughly; doing one practice is practicing one thing completely. Right here is the place, right here the way is realized. The place and way of realization are not distinct and apart, for their

realization manifests as one with the thorough mastery of the Buddhist teachings right here, right now.

The proof is in the pudding. Enlightenment is in what you do, what you say, and not just in a state of mind. This place and time, in each single thought, word and act, is the place where all is put into practice and realized. Enlightenment is not just a name or concept, but what you do and how you act and feel will manifest realization beyond any label. Whether you act with greed, anger, and division right here, or generosity, peace, and wholeness right here, is just up to what you choose to do in this moment.

Do not assume that what you realize becomes something you know or is perceived consciously as some state of "enlightenment." Although brought to realization immediately here and now, the mysterious state may not be apparent to the mind. Its realization may be beyond ordinary discriminating knowledge.

It is up to you to breathe life into wisdom, to make the unified whole show its face in this world of separation, to bring a touch of beauty to a planet of frequent ugliness, to manifest peace for a human race that swings between peace and war. We can always do something, big or small, to make things better. Wholeness, beauty, and peace are always present, like the moon hidden beyond the horizon. But it is up to you, me, and each of us to uncover them and manifest them in this life.

Here is a story that Dōgen tells:

Zen Master Baoche of Mt. Mayu was fanning himself. A young monk came before him and asked, "Master, the nature of air is always present and there is no place where it does not reach. Why then do you fan yourself?"

"Although you may know that the nature of the air is always present," Master Baoche replied, "you have not understood the meaning of its reaching everywhere."

The monk asked further, "Then what is the meaning of its reaching everywhere, Master?"

The master just carried on fanning himself. The monk bowed deeply.

Like the invisible air that is everywhere, you must fan to feel the air and let it move. It is up to you whether you fan up a cool and refreshing breeze or hot flames that burn down everything in their path.

Dōgen closes his letter with these words:

> The verification of the Buddhist teachings, the vivid means of their correct transmission, is just like this. We need to work to make it appear in life. If you believe that you can do without fanning because the air is always present, you will understand neither "always present" nor the nature of air. The nature of air is present always, thus the wind of the Buddha's house is a treasure like gold from the earth, turning its long rivers into sweet cream.

Enlightenment, like gold in the earth, is always present but in need of your digging hands to be revealed. It is like cream that is ever plentiful but needs our churning and skimming effort to let it rise and make it sweet. Then, the treasure is ours and we are nourished. Only then might we realize the truth right here.

Dōgen then dates his letter:

> Written in mid-autumn, the first year of Tempuku (1233), and given to my lay student Koshu Yō of Kyushu Island. Revised in the fourth year of Kenchō (1252).

Dōgen wrote to his student far away and long ago. However, he also writes to us here and now. "Genjō Kōan" lays out the fundamental vision of the great dance, which, as we shall see, Dōgen further explores in his many other writings.

# Samādhi That Is the King of Samādhis

Let us further explore the radical nature of Master Dōgen's zazen, the centerpiece of Dōgen's dance. We'll hear ol' Dōgen take up his jazz horn, really riffing on the sounds of shikantaza. It is a music and dance that echoes right through our life concerns.

We live in a day and age in which so many of us are always running, rarely satisfied, critical of life and others, and doubtful of our own self-worth. We may feel cut off from life, confused about our place in the world, alienated from other people. We are overwhelmed by the choices we need to make and the demands that society places upon us. It was certainly true for people in Dōgen's day and in the Buddha's time, but it's perhaps truer now than ever before.

For such dis-ease, Master Dōgen offers shikantaza as a timeless medicine. It is the medicine of just sitting, stopping the running for a while, then getting up to move again with stillness now in our hearts. It is the medicine we encountered earlier in his "Fukan Zazengi" and "Genjō Kōan." It is the medicine of seeing life, others, and ourselves each as a shining jewel, perfectly glimmering despite the many flaws that we seek to polish and remove. It is the medicine of connection and union for our feeling of disconnection. It is the medicine of taking care in our work and obligations, being sincere and diligent, yet not a prisoner of outcomes. It is the medicine of total awareness of the wholeness of this life, knowing that our place in the world is right here and now, no matter where life takes us. It is the medicine of knowing that, regardless of how many choices we need to make and how many demands are placed upon us, there is nothing ever lacking, no choice that is ever mistaken, nothing to achieve and no place to go to.

Dōgen taught that the practice of zazen is doing one act in one moment, with the deep feeling that that one act is the only one we need to do in that moment. When we act this way, we feel thoroughly connected and have a subtle sense that, as we do what we're doing, it is the whole world acting through us, *as* us.

To understand this way of experiencing things, let us study "Zanmai-O-Zanmai" (Samādhi That Is the King of Samādhis), another one of Dōgen's writings in which he speaks of zazen as the centerpiece of our Zen practice and all of life. As he often does, Dōgen makes the point in vivid and powerful language that we sit zazen because Buddhas sit in peace and contentment, and that our sitting thus embodies all Buddhas sitting. Even if we don't always feel this, we should sit with the faith that it is so. Then, rising up from our sitting cushions, that same attitude of doing the tasks that life presents in each moment, that same sensation of the whole world acting through us, that same satisfaction in just doing what we need to do in each instant, can travel with us through all life's busy days.

Besides our inability to rest in wholeness and contentment during our busy lives, another existential dis-ease that plagues human beings is a feeling of alienation from and conflict with the world. For this disease, Master Dōgen offers the medicine of radical connection and union.

Buddhists have a vision—as strange as it sounds—that everything is permeated by everything, and is easily and comfortably held within each and every other thing. The masters of the Huayan Buddhist school, an ancient Chinese tradition also known as the "Flower Garland" teachings, so influential on generations of Zen practitioners, believed that every thing in the universe is mutually creating, and in turn is being mutually created by, every other thing. Thus every drop of the ocean holds and creates the whole ocean and every grain of sand contains and shapes the entire world.

A magnificent image from the Huayan teachings is Indra's Net of jewels. Picture a vast net representing the whole universe, arising from the singularity that was the Big Bang and that spread out in all directions after its birth. At every one of countless points where the threads of the net meet, an iridescent jewel is set. Imagine that each jewel reflects all the jewels around it, and that each of those jewels in turn reflects the light from all the other jewels around it, on and on forever. This means that every single jewel is reflecting the reflections of all the other reflections upon reflections, near and far, of the whole body of jewels in the net. So each jewel—each particular entity or event in the universe—ultimately reflects and expresses the radiance of the entire universe and all within it. The totality can be seen in each of its parts, and each part is held safely in all other parts too. (I have a physicist friend who tells me that the fields of gravity that span the universe are not unlike this. Every bit of matter exerts a gravitational pull, great or small, on every other bit of matter, near or far.)

Buddhists recognize that every phenomenon in the universe, every stone or bird or flower or person of this world, is like one of those jewels in Indra's Net. Each jewel is a jewel in itself. A jewel may be flawed, a mirror can be cracked, a bird poor at flying, a flower might be missing petals, and a person can exist with any number of character faults and imperfections, yet they are all still jewels. Thus, a mirror with a crack is perfectly a cracked mirror, a poorly flying bird is precisely a bird that cannot fly well, a torn flower is impeccably a torn flower, and the same is true for flawed human beings. You and I are simply two shining jewels of you and I-ness, without one chip to add or take away to make that jewel more of a jewel. The world is a jewel too.

Not only is every inch, every atom of the universe fully manifesting every other inch and atom of the universe in this very moment, but all the past and any future to come is all fully held right here too. It is like saying that, if the universe is a great hourglass with sand falling to mark the passing of time, then the hourglass fully holds the past, the future, and the tiny point of now where one passes into the other. That is true even if the future, the way the sands will eventually fall, is still largely undetermined.

Which brings us back to zazen.

I can try to describe with words this picture of a unified universe, but unless we actually sit and taste the sweetness of this truth, it will be nothing more than words on paper. So it is vital that when we sit a moment of zazen, we sit as one of those jewels of Indra's Net holding all the other jewels, all the universe, and each inch and atom in it—all of this fully and flawlessly held within our posture of zazen. We sit as the hourglass, each grain of sand holding all other grains and the center point where time passes.

How beautiful it is to experience that every grain of sand and every moment of time is the vast sweep of things. We sit as the hourglass that is beyond time yet contains all of time, that remains unchanged as time seems to flow, ongoing even as things appear to come and go, to be born, and to die. We sit as the sitting jewel, single and unique yet simultaneously the whole reflecting the whole. We sit as the dance of the universe dancing as us, we sit as musicians of the universe playing the note of all notes, which is zazen. When we sit in such a way, in the total wholeness of sitting, nothing in life is lacking. This zazen is the medicine that Dōgen prescribed for the dissatisfaction that in Buddhism we refer to as suffering.

We don't have to look far in Dōgen's writings to find his exaltation of zazen, for he never failed to highlight the marvel and majesty of sitting itself. A prime example is this beautiful essay, "Zanmai-O-Zanmai" (The Samādhi That Is the King of Samādhis). I would like to go through it with you, for it is all about the profound interconnection that is zazen.

Before we get started, however, I do want to point out that this is one essay where Dōgen's wild use of language is clearly evident. So please remember to think of him as an expressive teacher who bent and wilded various images and expressions common in standard Mahayana and Zen Buddhist teachings to bring special feeling and power to them.

Dr. Hee-jin Kim summarizes Dōgen's intent this way:

> Throughout the *Shōbōgenzō*, Dōgen painstakingly dissects a given passage and explores its semantic possibilities at every turn, literally turning the conventional diction upside down and inside out. The result is a dramatic shift in our perception and understanding of the original passage. One of the most rewarding aspects of translating Dōgen's *Shōbōgenzō* is his radical challenge to ordinary language. To Dōgen the manner of expression is as important as the substance of thought; in fact, the experimentation with language is equivalent to the making of reality. Furthermore, Dōgen frequently puts forth deliberate, often brilliant, "misinterpretations" of certain notions and passages of Buddhism. This distortion of original meaning is not due to any ignorance of Chinese or Japanese (indeed, it testifies to a unique mastery of both) but rather to a different kind of thinking—the logic of the Buddhadharma."[3]

So, with this in mind, let us dig into Dōgen's "Samādhi That Is the King of Samādhis," Dōgen's word-jazz that expresses the dance of the universe, which is held within the pure action of zazen. He begins:

> To transcend all realms of the universe at once, to live a greatly honored life within the house of the Buddhas and Ancestors, is to be sitting in the lotus posture. To tread over the heads of followers of wrong paths and the legions pursuing evil ways, to become a true person in the inner

> sanctum of the Buddhas and Ancestors, this is sitting in
> the lotus posture. To transcend the extremes of the high-
> est supremacy of the Buddhas and Ancestors is just this
> one truth. Thus, this is the only practice that the Buddhas
> and Ancestors practice, and there is no other thing to do.

Dōgen begins by celebrating the superlative nature of the act of sitting with crossed legs. He pulls no punches. The sitting of zazen transcends all realms of the universe, is honored living in the home of the
Buddhas and Ancestors, and defeats all erroneous and evil beliefs. It is
a true act making a true person. It is the one practice that Buddhas
and Ancestors practice, and there is nothing more to do besides it.
Thus, we should sit zazen as an act transcendent of all the world, as
sitting inside Buddha's house, the one path to follow.

> We should realize that the universe in sitting is far different
> from other universes. Clarifying this principle, Buddhist
> Ancestors resolve and realize the aspiration to first practice,
> the practice itself, the state of awakening, and the final nir-
> vana of the Buddhas and Ancestors.

The world experienced before sitting and the world experienced
during and after sitting are very different. It is the same world, yet
both our experience and expression are not the same as before sitting.
We are always Buddha, originally enlightened, but one view is awakened to that fact and one is not. With that truth in mind, the Buddhas and Ancestors resolve to first begin to practice, then they practice, awaken, and pass away at the end of their earthly lives. Awakening
can happen while alive, but when a Buddha dies he or she is said to
enter "final nirvana." (Actually, "enter" is not really the right term, for
this is "return" in death to the wholeness that has been present all
along, and which we have never left at all, although we may falsely
have felt separate during life.) In the former we realize the world beyond

division while still alive in this world of division, but upon death and the end of the body, there is no division at all.

Dōgen also emphasizes in other essays in *Shōbōgenzō* that every step up the mountain is the mountain, that all aspects of awakening and Buddha—from the first thought of practice, to practice, awakening, and passing away—don't turn us into anything we were not all along. However, awakening to that fact makes things very different. Thus the same universe before and during sitting is known very differently. We were always Buddha, we were always this universe expressing itself, but we just did not know it. Now, seeing what was always so, we gain nothing that was not always so except this seeing and understanding. Thus, the beginner and the advanced practitioner are the same—all Buddha through and through—but hopefully the advanced practitioner sees it more clearly and lives in accordance with that fact.

> We inquire and explore whether, in the moment of our sitting, all realms are vertical. Or are they horizontal? In the moment of our sitting, what is this sitting itself? Is it a somersault? Is it a state of vigorous and lively activity? Is it thinking? Is it not thinking? Is it making something? Is it not making something? Are we sitting inside of sitting? Is it sitting inside of bodymind? Are we sitting having dropped away "inside of sitting," "inside of bodymind," and so on? We should inquire and explore thousands, tens of thousands, of points such as these.

We are asked to ponder these questions about zazen, though not by actually thinking about these things during zazen itself, where we inquire not by pondering, but by simply sitting and experiencing. I believe that Dōgen is pointing us to zazen as an action beyond all opposites and dichotomies, yet embodying them as well. Zazen encompasses and transcends all such partial views as horizontal versus vertical, stillness and movement, thinking and not thinking. Zazen is precisely all those categories, but is also free of them. The back is vertical, the legs horizontal, yet zazen embodies all directions (in Zen parlance, "horizontal" and "vertical" also stand for undivided and divided views). Zazen is sitting that contains both stillness and movement because it contains all the activity of the world. It is the realization of Buddha by not trying to realize or make Buddha. It is the non-thinking that is neither thinking nor not thinking.

In sitting, we step beyond tens of thousands of other questions and dichotomies. We sit for a long or short time—both of which are timeless. A Buddha is beyond all division and comparison, yet embodies this world of division and comparison. In this way, sitting zazen is the completeness of the jewel that runs right through all human views of completion or incompletion, perfection or imperfection.

Another traditional image from Huayan Buddhism says that if gold is cast into either a beautiful or ugly statue, gold is still manifesting in both, beyond beautiful and ugly. The human eye and mind judge beauty. Our zazen is sitting as the goldness of the gold that transcends all dichotomies.

> Sit in the lotus posture with the body, sit in the lotus posture with the mind. We should sit in the lotus posture with bodymind dropped away.

Among all the dichotomies to be encompassed and transcended in zazen is the question of whether we are a body and mind sitting zazen, or whether there is just sitting that is sitting beyond body and mind. We are a mind that sits, we are a body that sits. Truly, zazen has both aspects of body sitting and mind sitting. We sit with a stable and balanced posture pouring our "self" into the body, losing and rediscovering ourselves in the body just as a dancer whose body is absorbed in dance. Zazen is a bodily activity. But it's also a mental activity. In zazen, the mind is balanced and stable, not tangled in thoughts, resting in the wisdom that shines through views. Yet, when we drop all dichotomies, divisive thoughts, and judgments, and sit with the body comfortable and balanced, we might say that the mind is then at rest, and the body is "paid no nevermind." At such a point there is just "bodymind dropped away."

> My late master, the Old Buddha, said, "Practicing Zen is body and mind dropped off. Just to sit shikantaza is to attain from the beginning; it is not necessary to burn incense, make prostrations, recite the Buddha's name, practice repentance, or read and chant scriptures."

Once again, we find Dōgen's emphasis that shikantaza is enlightenment from the very first moment of sitting. It is "to attain from the beginning," whether or not we realize it. The shining moon is not made by our seeing it, and enlightenment is not dependent on our realizing it. Trust in Buddha seen or unseen, even in the darkest and stormiest moments of life.

Dōgen also says that zazen is the only practice we need to do. However, scholars who have reviewed his extensive writings have noted that, in fact, he did undertake other activities like burning incense, bowing, reciting the names of various Buddhas, reflecting on the precepts, and studying or chanting various sutras. His teacher in China, Master Rújìng, did as well. Thus, what Dōgen surely meant by these words is that zazen is the only practice, complete and whole, *while sitting*. While sitting, there is no before or after. But later, when getting up from the cushion and engaging another practice, we can bring that same sense of zazen to all actions. When lighting incense, there is only lighting incense; likewise when bowing, chanting, cleaning the temple, and so forth.

The same wisdom can be brought outside the monastery too. When changing diapers, there is only changing diapers. This is also the attainment of enlightenment from the beginning. If your job is handling test tubes in a research lab or radiators in a garage, there is only handling test tubes or radiators—each is the one thing to do in that moment. Each itself is sitting in the Buddha's eye, which sees no distinctions and in which all is sacred.

This does not mean that we must do those actions always "mindfully," absorbed in just that one action without thinking about anything else. People sometimes think that Zen practice is about always focusing on one thing in one moment, to the exclusion of everything else. I do not feel that is realistic or even healthy. The moon is always shining, seen or unseen. We do not need to be staring at the moon in each instant in order to make it more the moon. Thus, sometimes the "one thing" of a moment is actually a few things at once, and they are the moment too. We confuse being present and mindful in the moment ("When drinking tea, just drink tea") with being at one with the moment (allowing and merging with conditions of life just as they are). While the former is a healthy exercise to undertake at certain times, whether a monk writing with a brush, a painter painting, or a parent playing with her kids in the park, it is not realistic for most of us to focus so intensely most of the time. It's not even realistic for busy monks who must often juggle their ceremonies, guests, budget concerns, and travel plans like any other professional. So, when drinking tea, if you are a bit worried about tomorrow's work project, just drink tea and be worried about the project. That is what is happening in the present, sacred moment.

Nonetheless, when the bell rings to indicate the beginning of zazen, put the planning and concerns, the diapers and teacups, down. Don't burn incense or make prostrations. Before or after zazen is the time for all that. At the time of zazen, just sit zazen.

> Clearly, for the last four or five hundred years, my former master is the only one who has plucked out the eye of the Buddhas and Ancestors and sits within the eye of the Buddhas and Ancestors. There are very few of equal stature even in the land of China. It is rare to have clarified that sitting is the Buddhadharma, that the Buddhadharma is the act of sitting. Even if some have realized sitting to be

the Buddhadharma, they have not realized sitting as sitting. So how can the Buddhadharma thus be maintained as the Buddhadharma?

First, it is good to note that Dōgen appreciated his teacher, Master Rújìng, calling him the "Old Buddha" and proclaiming that he was the best in all of China. This may be due to the fact that both Rújìng and Dōgen had a unique, radical approach to "just sitting." They proclaimed a non-utilitarian approach to sitting, a pathless path to realizing the mind of a Buddha which rests whole and complete in this moment and action. Such a style of meditation is very rare, if not unique, in Buddhism.

Most forms of meditation, including other styles of Zen meditation, have as their goal finding Buddha or enlightenment at some point in the distant future, or to reach some special experience or deep concentration. Shikantaza is unique in positing that we are already at home and always have been. We realize this when we stop traveling and searching, and see that each moment is already total arrival. The most "special experience" is to radically drop all hunt and thirst for some other "special experience."

It is a unique philosophy, certainly meriting Dōgen's comment that his teacher was sitting inside the eye of the Buddhas and Ancestors, realizing sitting as the Buddhadharma, Buddha's truth, and the Buddha's truth as just sitting.

This being said, there is sitting of the mind, which is not the same as sitting of the body. There is sitting of the body, which is not the same as sitting of the mind. There is sitting of the body and mind dropped away, which is not the same as sitting of the body and mind dropped away. To have attained the state like this is the accordance of the practice and realization of the Buddhas and Ancestors. Take close care of the thoughts, ideas, and perceptions; explore thoroughly this mind, will, and consciousness.

This passage is open to interpretation, and it often strikes commentators as being somewhat vague. I will offer my own view, expanding on my earlier comments about sitting of the body, sitting of the mind, and sitting of bodymind dropped away. Zazen is a kind of yoga, a joining of body and mind in which the entirety of body and mind is engaged. Body and mind are "not two"; that is why we can call them "bodymind." That being said, there is a physical component to zazen. We sit as best we can in a balanced, stable, and still posture which nurtures a balanced, stable, and still state of mind, the mental component of zazen.

In the same vein, various physical activities can be considered a kind of "moving Zen"—martial arts, tea ceremony, dance, and the like. We can lose ourselves in them and find a new, expansive sense of self that feels like an embodying of wholeness. Any action, such as sweeping the floor or even making toast, if we truly pour ourself into the motion, can be approached in this way. My teacher, Nishijima Roshi, was a long-distance runner in his youth, and he compared the physical and mental balance of running to aspects of zazen, as the body simply takes over and carries you along in harmony as you run. Sitting in the balanced, stable, comfortable posture of zazen is supposed to have a similar effect. We are able to drop away all thoughts of the body in that posture, much as a runner drops the body in her running or a dancer in his dancing. They become so at one with the body and the action that the body is dropped from awareness. This is zazen of the body.

In the mental component to zazen we do not grab onto thoughts, do not engage in judgments, and sit in the wholeness and completeness of zazen itself. We experience "goallessness" and the realization of "nothing more to attain, no other place to go." This is zazen of the mind.

However, there is also zazen in which both body and mind (or bodymind) are dropped away. The mind is spacious, the body is stable and balanced. The hard borders between the self and the rest of life soften and sometimes fully drop away. To realize this state is "the accordance of the practice and realization of the Buddhas and Ancestors." In other words, the doing of zazen is the realization of zazen.

The sentence "There is sitting of the body and mind dropped away, which is not the same as sitting of the body and mind dropped away" is a bit confusing. According to Nishijima Roshi and others, it may mean that the mere intellectual idea of this dropping is not the same as the actual doing and experiencing of dropping.

The next line is even more confusing at first sight: "Take close care of the thoughts, ideas, and perceptions; explore thoroughly this mind, will, and consciousness." I believe that Dōgen's meaning is that we should be on guard of our thinking, ideation, and perception, and understand well our mind, will, and consciousness, in order to not get caught up in them—in other words, we must transcend our mental claptrap. In other writings, Dōgen includes lists of mental operations like these and urges us to cease and desist from them or, at least, to not wallow in or become tangled by them.

For example, in "Fukan Zazengi," Dōgen writes: "Think of neither good nor bad, right nor wrong. Stop the whirling wheels of mind, will, and consciousness, cease the measures and judgments of your inner thoughts, ideas, and perceptions." This use of "stop" and "cease" is not taken by most Zen teachers to mean a total stopping of thought as if in a coma or deep trance, but simply our not stirring up and not being caught in those perceptions, thoughts, and emotions that naturally float through the mind during zazen. This also seems to be Dōgen's meaning in his advice in the above passage to "take close care of" the thoughts, ideas, and perceptions. Thoughts may come and go, but we see through and past them to discover the clarity and wholeness of reality that underlies our perception of a separate and divided world, Thus, in another text, "Gakudō Yōjinshū," Dōgen states:

> Mind, will, and consciousness are not primary; thoughts, ideas, and perceptions are not primary. Without using any of these, one enters the Buddha Way by arranging body and mind.

Dōgen seems clear that we are to go past or become untangled from these mental processes and operations during zazen.

> The Buddha Śākyamuni addressed a great assembly, saying, "If we sit with legs crossed, then the bodymind will realize samādhi; the dignity and virtue of this state will be revered by the multitudes. Just as the sun lights up the world, the dullness, laziness, and indolence that cloud the mind are removed, and the body is made light and not dull. Awareness is likewise light and supple. You sit calmly like a coiled dragon. On seeing even a picture of someone sitting crossed-legged, King Māra (the demon king of delusion) is frightened. How much more on actually seeing someone sitting stably without leaning or stirring, realizing the truth.

This passage, with minor differences, is from the *Treatise on the Great Perfection of Wisdom* (In Chinese, the *Dazhidu lun*), a sutra most cherished in Chinese Buddhism. Unlike the common meaning of samādhi as a state of intense concentration, Dōgen's description describes a state of mind that is light, clear, calm, and supple. The power of Māra—the symbol for confused and negative mental states such as dullness and indolence—is dispelled by sitting. Further, the act of zazen itself is a sacred and dignified action. Beyond the mental ease we may experience in zazen, sitting itself is a sacred act of limitless virtue, as Dōgen next explains:

> So, on seeing a picture of the lotus posture, even King Māra, the demon king of delusion, is surprised and frightened. How much more when we are actually sitting with legs crossed; the virtue is beyond imagination. This being the case, the virtue of our everyday sitting is limitless.
> The Buddha Śākyamuni addressed a great assembly, saying (in the *Treatise on the Great Perfection of Wisdom*),

"This is why we sit with legs crossed." Further, the Tathāgata, the World Honored One, teaches his disciples that they should sit like this, [saying that] some groups of non-Buddhists seek the way by continuously standing with one leg raised, or seek the way by always standing, or seek the way by wrapping their legs on their shoulders. Through wrong practices like these, their minds are crazed, sink into a sea of delusion, and their bodies are not left in peace. For this reason, the Buddha teaches his disciples to sit cross-legged, sitting with the mind upright. Why? Because when the body is upright, the mind is easily set right. When the body sits upright, the mind will not be sluggish. With upright mind and correct mental attitude, the attention is placed on what's just present before us. If the mind is agitated or distracted, or if the body leans, adjust them and bring them back. When we want to experience samādhi, want to enter samādhi, we gather the various wandering thoughts, the distracting images. Practicing like this, we realize and enter the samādhi that is king of samādhis.

Here too, we see Dōgen recommending zazen as a practice because it is the practice of the Buddhas. He contrasts it with various ascetic and yogic practices found in India where sāddhus or holy men would practice keeping an arm raised over their head for decades, for example, or stand on one leg. The Buddha's way was more moderate. Dōgen emphasizes the wholeness of body and mind, where an upright and stable body facilitates an upright and stable mind.

Once again, we see that Dōgen does not speak of samādhi as a deep state of concentration, but as a mind without agitation or distraction in which the attention is placed on what is present before us. I would call this "open spacious awareness"—a mind state in which we witness in equanimity what is present in our environment, as well as the thoughts that pass through our minds. We are present, upright, alert, and undisturbed by what we see. If we become tangled in such thoughts or emotions, agitated or distracted, we gently come back to this open awareness again and again. Dōgen continues:

> Clearly, we know that sitting with legs crossed is the samādhi that is king of samādhis, its realization and entry. All the samādhis are the servants of this king samādhi. To sit with legs crossed is the body set straight, is the mind set straight, is the bodymind set straight, is the straight Buddhas and Ancestors, straight realization and experience, receiving straight, the straight pinnacle, the straight vital bloodline of the lineage.
>
> Now, crossing the legs of the human skin, flesh, bones, and marrow, we are the samādhi that is king of samādhis. The World Honored One is always maintaining and safeguarding this sitting with legs crossed. To his disciples he authentically transmits sitting with legs crossed. To both humans and gods he teaches this sitting with legs crossed. The mind seal that is authentically transmitted by the Seven Buddhas is just this.

Dōgen emphasizes that this sitting with crossed legs is the whole works by saying, for example, that this sitting is, itself, straight realization and experience. It is itself the "skin, flesh, bones, and marrow" of this way of sitting. He is referring to an old kōan in which Bodhidharma tells four of his disciples that they have gained understanding of various levels, corresponding to the depth from skin to marrow. Yet, in his writings, Dōgen emphasized that zazen transcends all concepts of shallow and deep, and is marrow to skin all at once. It is, in fact, the flowing bloodline of the Seven Buddhas, who in Mahayana Buddhism are said to have been the Seven Buddhas of the past leading up to Śākyamuni in this world. Crossing the legs (or sitting and even reclining in another stable posture when necessary) is a sacred happening. Balancing and straightening body and mind, attaining clarity and insight and a sense of peace and wholeness, are at the heart of our practice. Yet all of these arise from not seeking and simply sitting in the completion, wholeness, and sacredness of sitting for the sake of sitting.

Do not neglect Dōgen's message that merely sitting, crossing the legs, is the World Honored One sitting. From the point of view of shikantaza, it is a mistake to meditate for some goal of peace or concentration that leaves out the radical non-attainment and sacred self-fulfillment of just sitting.

Dōgen goes on:

> Śākyamuni Buddha, sitting with legs crossed under the bodhi tree, passes fifty minor kalpas, passes sixty kalpas, passes countless kalpas. Sitting with legs crossed for three weeks [the time the Buddha was said to have sat in meditation under the bodhi tree before his enlightenment] or sitting cross-legged for just one moment is the turning of the wondrous Dharma wheel, is the Buddha's teachings of a lifetime. There is nothing lacking. This is the yellow rolls and vermillion rollers [which hold the scrolls of all the sutras and commentaries on Buddhist doctrine ever written]. Buddha meeting Buddha is just this moment. This is precisely the time when living beings become Buddhas.

Dōgen emphasizes how moments of sitting zazen transcend time itself. Each instant encompasses many *kalpas*, the Sanskrit term for long eons of cosmic time that are beyond measure. Each moment of sitting is the turning of the wondrous wheel of the Dharma—that is, all teachings proclaimed. We must sit shikantaza zazen with the attitude that each one moment of sitting fully embodies and also transcends all the countless eons of time, is the silent preaching, hearing, and fruition of all the Buddha's teachings. It is Buddha meeting Buddha on the zafu; it is precisely all Buddhas sitting.

The First Ancestor in China, the venerable Bodhidharma, upon coming from India in the West, passed nine years in zazen with legs crossed facing a wall at Shaolin monastery at the Shaoshi mountain peak. Thereafter, his head and eyes [of wisdom and insight] have continued to pervade the land of China. The vital lifeblood of the First Ancestor is just this sitting with legs crossed. Before the First Ancestor came from the West, the people of eastern lands [knew various kinds of meditation and Buddhist philosophy, but] never knew [true] sitting with legs crossed. Only since the ancestral master came from the West have they known it.

Therefore, whether for one life or for ten thousand lives, from head to tail, without leaving the temple where you are, just sitting day and night with legs crossed, without any other practices: this is the samādhi that is king of all samādhis.

These words, written in 1244 in old Japan, are the medicine for our human suffering today wherever we are. Dōgen speaks of not needing to leave the temple, but we can see the inch of ground where we find ourselves as the temple that we need not leave. How wonderful to know that the promised land is not in another place but right where we sit or stand.

# One Bright Pearl

IKKA MYŌJU

The next two sections of *Shōbōgenzō* look outward from zazen toward the wholeness of the universe and the unity of being and time. Although in fact, there is no looking "outward" or "inward," for zazen itself encompasses the wholeness of the universe, and is all being-time. Being-time is just the wholeness, and the wholeness is zazen. As we sit, we sit with all the universe, all things, past, present, or future flowing in and out of our zazen, and zazen is the center of it all.

So, let us now speak of the wholeness of the universe, which Master Dōgen compares to a great shining jewel whose countless facets are all the many things of the world. Why is it important for us to develop the wisdom to know this jewel-like quality of the world?

As I have emphasized many times in this book, each event within this jewel, this world, both welcome and unwelcome, can be encountered as its own jewel. The cosmos is a jewel that holds all of us, and every star or grain of dust is a radiant jewel too. Jewels within jewels— some flawed, perhaps—but who is to say that any of them are less than priceless? It is important, especially when we face the hard times in life, that we learn to understand this fact. We must learn to encounter all facets of this world, and all moments of our life, as shining jewels.

The story begins like this, on a river:

> In this world of ours, in the great Song Empire of China, at Xuanshashan in Fuzhou province, once lived a certain great master named Xuansha, also known by his ordinary name of Shibei. Before he became a monk, he loved fishing, and would float down the Nantai River, doing just what fishermen do. He never expected to encounter the golden fish that jumps in the boat by itself without being fished.

Dōgen's opening describes Shibei, later known as Xuansha, floating down life's river, working hard yet accepting things as they come. It seems that Shibei, even before he became a monk, had a very accepting attitude toward life. At the same time, he never expected life to just toss good things his way—he never thought that a golden fish would simply jump in his boat.

But finally he started to have questions about the meaning of it all. Maybe he felt that the years were growing short (thirty was quite old back then). So, he went looking for the truth:

> One day, at the start of the Xiantong era [ninth century], he suddenly desired to leave his boat and his secular life behind and become a monk. He was thirty years of age when he realized the precariousness of this fleeting world and the preciousness of the Buddha Way.
>
> At last, he climbed Mt. Xuefeng to join the order of the Great Master of Xuefeng, also known as Zhenjue, day and night endeavoring on the way. Then one day, after some time, wishing to explore widely so as to deepen his understanding, he left the mountain carrying his traveling bag, planning to visit other monasteries. But as he walked down

the mountain, he stubbed his toe on a rock and it began to bleed. Blood flowing and in great pain, he had a sudden realization and said to himself, "It is said that this body does not truly exist, so where does this pain come from?" Thereupon, he returned to Zhenjue, and Master Zhenjue asked him, "What is it, Ascetic Bei [for Shibei was known for his hard practice]?" Shibei said, "In the end, I cannot be deceived by others." Master Zhenjue appreciated these words, and answered, "Is there anyone who does not always possess these words, yet who else can express them?"

"Yet who else can express them?" means that we must embody this truth personally; we cannot rely on ideas we have encountered, or words we have heard spoken by others. Only you can express this truth for yourself, and you have to feel it profoundly within yourself. Shibei tried to go here and there in search of the truth, seeking liberation from human suffering, but he stumbled on the truth that is never far away. In this case, he experienced a little pain, which awakened him to the fact that there was no place to go in search of the treasure he had possessed all along. He became a monk just to realize that this truth had been present in his fishing boat too.

Shibei's painful toe reflects another kōan, this time about a painful nose:

> Master Shigong Huizang asked Zhigong, "Do you know the way to grasp emptiness?"
> Zhigong said, "Yes, I do know the way to grasp emptiness."
> Shigong said, "So, how do you grasp it?"
> Zhigong clutched at the air with his hands.
> Shigong said, "Then you don't really know how to grasp emptiness."
> Zhigong responded, "How do you grasp it?"
> Shigong stuck his fingers into Zhigong's nostrils and gave his nose a yank.

Zhigong shouted in pain, "Ouch! You are hurting my nose!"

Shigong said, "This is how to grasp emptiness."

Emptiness is the flowing wholeness that manifests as each of us and as all things. We each are here, yet we are also the flowing wholeness, just as each falling droplet is the waterfall, or each dancer is the dance. We call it emptiness because these seemingly solid bodies and objects around us are, from another perspective, empty of solidity and independent existence.

Buddhism teaches that this body and all the things of the world have a dreamlike quality to them—each is a passing, illusory expression of the dancing flow of emptiness, wholeness. Yet, dream or not, that dream sometimes hurts! Flowing wholeness or not, blood sometimes flows from a cut in one's throbbing foot.

Even modern science has demonstrated that much of our experience of the world—and our self identity in relationship to it—is actually a virtual (and very subjective) recreation put together by the gray matter between our ears to give meaning to the raw data that comes in through our senses. Before moving on to Dōgen's thirteenth-century vision of the dream, it is worth taking a moment to look at this a bit more closely.

It is now well understood that you and me, the trees and the most distant stars, are all made of the same elements, the same matter and energy, the same star dust. Biologists and physicists will point out that we are not only individuals, but integral components and expressions of larger ecologies, systems, and fields. One might say that we are just facets of this planet and of the whole universe that have come alive in a certain time and place under particular conditions. Much as a leaf of a tree is not only a single leaf but is also a vital aspect of the tree itself—which in turn is a key element of an entire forest, a food chain, an ecosystem made up of matter and energy come together in particular forms, of atoms and molecules arranged in unbroken energy fields—there is more to us than just our individuality.

However, sense data, which gives rise to tastes, tactile sensations, sights, smells, and sounds, comes in through our sense organs and is processed by our brains, which proceed to organize the information, drawing borders, sorting into categories, assigning names, imposing judgments. From all this we form a virtual experience based on what the brain has decided is important and what it chooses to ignore. The fact is, you have never actually experienced holding your child or your lover, never truly tasted the sweetness of ice cream, never really felt the pain of a stubbed toe apart from the amazing show in your cerebral cortex that fashions children and lovers, sweetness and ice cream, toes and pain.

There is nothing in science that prevents each of us from knowing ourselves as more than isolated individuals, and much that allows us to know ourselves as singular expressions of encompassing wholes. We are not only creatures on this planet but, in a true sense, we are this planet come alive to walk and talk under particular conditions that came to be "us."

But don't just listen to my words: you have to know this truth yourself. You must experience the flowing wholeness, sense the dreamlike quality of our separation, feel the wetness of the waters of the river that you are, know the heat and energy of the vibrant dance moving through you. Zazen, and all our practice, is the means by which we learn this lesson deep in our real-unreal bones.

In this case, a stubbed toe brought Shibei a clear realization. Maybe some pain or crisis in your life can do the same for you.

> Then Zhenjue queried, "Why are you not off on your pilgrimage?"
>
> Master Xuansha [Shibei] responded, "Bodhidharma did not come to China, the Second Ancestor did not go to India."
>
> Zhenjue praised this.

Zen legend relates that Master Bodhidharma did, in fact, travel to China in order to bring Zen over from India. However, the Second

Ancestor, Master Huike, never went to India. Xuansha would know this, yet he says that neither Bodhidharma nor the Second Ancestor came nor went. I take Master Xuansha's response to mean that, going or not going, there is truth always already right here.

Xuansha (Shibei) came to intimately know this suchness, which comes and goes, yet is also beyond all coming and going. As Dōgen taught in "Fukan Zazengi," "There is no reason to leave your own sitting place and make aimless trips to dusty foreign lands. When your first step is mistaken, you will stumble right past the great way that is immediately before you."

Dōgen continues Xuansha's story:

> Before, in his life as a fisherman, Master Xuansha had never seen sutras or read [Buddhist] treatises even in his dreams. He just focused on his determination to practice, and his resolve was fully apparent. Zhenjue often praised Xuansha as the outstanding disciple of his order. His coarse cotton robe was well worn, but patched hundreds of times without being replaced. Next to his skin he wore only paper or mugwort grasses.
>
> Apart from his time with Zhenjue, he never did study with another. Thus, he did truly realize the power that he succeeded to through his master's teachings.
>
> After he had attained the way, Xuansha taught people by saying, "The whole universe in the ten directions is one bright pearl." One day, a monk asked him, "I have heard you say that the whole universe in the ten directions is one bright pearl. How should I understand this?" The master responded, "The whole universe in the ten directions is one bright pearl. What use is understanding?" At a later time, the master asked the same question of this monk, "The whole universe in the ten directions is one bright pearl, how do you understand this?" The monk repeated, "The

whole universe in the ten directions is one bright pearl. What use is understanding?"

Master Xuansha responded, "I see that you are making a livelihood inside the demon's cave on the black mountain."

With his words, "What use is understanding?" Master Xuansha cautions the student that intellectual understanding separates the ponderer from the wholeness that is the one bright pearl. Some truths are best experienced intimately by a subtle knowing beyond analysis and conceptualization. Of course, thinking may be necessary and helpful sometimes, but ultimately it can get in the way.

The monk seems to only mouth the master's words. Xuansha criticizes this answer by saying that the student is living inside the "demon's cave on the black mountain." This is an oft-repeated Zen expression that indicates a student is attached to thinking or mere mimicry. As we shall see, however, Dōgen brings some light and life into this dark cave.

> This expression, "the whole universe in the ten directions is one bright pearl," originated with Master Xuansha. The point is that the whole universe in the ten directions is not vast and great, not minute and small, not square or round, neither crooked nor straight.

Dōgen describes the whole universe in the ten directions (meaning all points of the compass: east, west, north, south, the four points in between, and the zenith and nadir) as going beyond all limiting or opposing descriptions, while embodying each and all of them. What might he mean?

I am cautious in claiming that modern scientific ideas always back up Buddhism. It depends on which aspect of Buddhism one is discussing. For example, some traditional Buddhist beliefs may prove to be nothing more than superstition, just traditional ways of looking at the world that modern discoveries show to be unlikely. I believe that Buddhism, like all ancient religions, is filled with many old wives' tales and untenable claims scattered amid the solid truths.

I sometimes get more traditional Buddhists upset when I question their detailed descriptions of the mechanisms of rebirth after death, or the stories that claim amazing, superhuman qualities and powers for the Buddha and other Buddhist Ancestors. I am skeptical of their literal truth. I am open to the possibility of some form of rebirth, but I am doubtful of more detailed assertions of how that might work based on the evidence we now have.

I can approach many fanciful descriptions in Buddhism as psychologically meaningful myth or symbol, perhaps, but not as historical facts. Many supernatural or extraordinary religious claims strike me as stories that well-intentioned religious people have created to elevate the figures of Buddhism and their teachings. I believe that many of the more fantastic claims are likely just that: fantasy.

That does not mean that I believe science can have all the answers, by any means, for while a chemist or biologist might describe much about the chemical makeup of sugar and oral receptors, or the hormonal reactions of the body associated with love, neither can truly capture the subjective truth of sweetness experienced on the tongue, or the pangs of a mother's love for her child. Not even our greatest poets can fully portray the latter. There are aspects of Buddhist practice, however, that can work a revolution of the mind, changing how we taste the sweetness of life and allowing us to see the connection between us and the rest of the world as "not one, yet not two"—as a pregnant mother and her unborn child within. We can experience this way of being by a simple change in our way of thinking and self-definition. The model of self-identity that we create in the prefrontal cortex and other portions of the brain can be altered through zazen and Zen insights. We can realize that we do not end at the border of the skin, that the outside world flows in as we flow out, much as the oxygen and nutrition in the blood of the mother flow in and out of her child as one organic whole.

So it's true that science does not have all the answers. There are vast gaps in our knowledge, and scientific theories are frequently proven wrong. Hamlet said:

*There are more things in heaven and earth, Horatio,*
*Than are dreamt of in your philosophy.*

Our present certainty of what the world is and how it functions is necessarily incomplete, and is sometimes as wrong as the certainty of people of past centuries who had their own quaint beliefs about the workings of the world. Many of our current beliefs are also likely to be judged quaint by coming generations. We must keep an open mind to new ways of seeing. On the other hand, the fact that science does not have all the answers is no reason to run to the other extreme and to believe every wild supposition or miracle story of Buddhism or any other religion.

I do not believe that science and Buddhist beliefs need always cover the same ground, but neither need they conflict. Discoveries and theories of modern science can frequently be perfectly harmonious with, even supporting of, some traditional Buddhist views.

For example, Dōgen states, "The whole universe in the ten directions is not vast and great, not minute and small." Many physicists will point out that, if our universe was born in a singular Big Bang, and assuming that there is nothing outside the universe to compare the universe to, then the universe is beyond big or small, for there is no outside scale of measure. One can compare the size of a tree to a mountain that stands apart from the tree, but to what does one compare the size of the universe? We can say that the universe is vast compared to what it contains, such as our world or our single galaxy or a grain of sand. But we cannot say that the universe itself is big or small because there is nothing outside it to hold it up against. As some science fiction stories depict, our whole universe might be nothing more than an atom in a giant's kitchen table! Likewise, even if there are many universes upon universes, one cannot say that their totality is big or small if there is nothing beyond that totality to compare the total to. One can only say that the whole appears greater in scale than its constituent parts. But does this greatness extend to value or worth?

We may correctly note that an elephant is bigger than an ant because it has more mass or occupies more space. And we might note that a planet, a sun, or a whole galaxy is bigger than both ants and elephants. But there is no reason to assume, apart from human valuation, that a tiny ant is therefore less vital than an elephant. If it could be bothered with silly human questions, the ant might have its own opinion about what is most important.

Again, in our ordinary way of thinking, a ton of gold has more value than an ounce of gold or a clump of mud. Yet gold is neither the shiniest nor rarest metal on the periodic table. Only we humans can celebrate it as precious. From a Buddhist perspective, gold or a clump of mud are both equally a single precious jewel of equal infinite worth, and together they are also a single jewel of infinite worth. A single ant is a jewel of infinite worth, a whole ant colony is also a jewel of infinite worth, a planet or all the universe is also a jewel of infinite worth. You, dear reader, are one such jewel of infinite worth.

Dōgen said that the whole universe in the ten directions is "not square or round, neither crooked nor straight." In fact, it is so fluid in its makeup that it can assume all those qualities. Sometimes the universe forms into a square brick, sometimes into a round stone, sometimes something bent and sometimes something straight. It is sometimes blue and sometimes green or red (as interpreted by the cones and rods of our eyes), sometimes big and sometimes small.

In addition, appearances can be deceiving. Even children can spot optical illusions in which the mind is fooled, and round things and straight things, long things and short, are other than they seem. The earth appears flat, yet is a sphere; the sun seems to rise and set, yet it is the earth that is moving. Time is also now known to be relative, changing based on our position and motion. It is not absolute, as we once assumed.

Is the universe young or old? We speak of a universe that is approximately fourteen billion years old, and we measure distances in light years. But in geological terms, millions of years are just a blink of an eye. On the other end of the spectrum, how finely can a moment be divided?

Einstein has shown us that, at the event horizon of a black hole, time may appear to stop to outside observers. We now know that due to special relativity, were we able to approach the speed of light, the relative shape and length of objects would change radically and time would dilate. In general relativity, an apple's falling to the ground due to gravity is also the ground's rising up to the apple as space-time bends to meet it. (My friend in Australia often reminds me that his country is not really "down under," for there is nothing to prevent us from turning the world map upside down, nor any way to identify the top or bottom of the planet when it is just a ball hanging in empty space.)

The universe appears to be expanding, although perhaps not into anything, much as an origami flower opens into empty space. An unfolding piece of paper never gets any bigger as it unfolds, in the sense that it is just the same piece of paper that it was before. Someday, it is supposed, the universe will simply cool and fade back into oblivion, or perhaps other universes will follow upon universes (both Buddhism and modern science speak of the possibility for that). Much of this is still theory and speculation, but the point is that size, shape, distance, speed, and time are all relative concepts. We should not trust our so-called common sense about things like near and far, now and then, big and small, round and square. Truly, Dōgen was many hundreds of years ahead of his time in noting such facts about the universe.

In Xuansha and Dōgen's vision, all is one bright pearl, and every piece of the pearl is equally pearly. The one pearl is simultaneously manifesting as all the individual forms and colors, each equally majestic when perceived with a Buddha's eye. The one jewel is all things, which are each its own jewel and all the one jewel.

I am not an expert, but my physicist friend tells me that according to some theories, reality may be something like a hologram in which every part of the hologram fully contains all the rest in its entirety. Thus, if we were to cut off any corner of a hologram, we could still see the entire image through it. Every viewing angle offers the image in a different perspective but includes the entire object. Tiny grains of the universe can contain the whole universe. There are many representations of this in Mahayana literature. One is from the *Vimalakīrti Sutra*:

> The bodhisattva who lives in the inconceivable liberation can put the king of mountains, Sumeru, which is so high, so great, so noble, and so vast, into a mustard seed. He can perform this feat without enlarging the mustard seed and without shrinking Mount Sumeru. [ . . . ] Furthermore, reverend Śāriputra, the bodhisattva who lives in the inconceivable liberation can pour into a single pore of his skin all the waters of the four great oceans . . . (*The Holy Teaching of Vimalakīrti: A Mahayana Sutra*, translation by Robert Thurman pp. 52–53)

Who, then, can say that a single grain of sand or a single moment of time is finite? The grain contains all; each moment holds all time. It reminds me of Blake's famous lines:

> *To see a World in a Grain of Sand*
> *And a Heaven in a Wild Flower*
> *Hold Infinity in the palm of your hand*
> *And Eternity in an hour.*

We can come to feel this, see this, know this truth.

Thus, do not be so quick to judge a grain of sand as either big or small, a blade of grass as tall or short, a moment of time as long or brief, or the universe as vast and distant. It is also a mistake, my physicist friend tells me, to think of the universe as having a particular "center." Better said, each and every place is the center because the Big Bang happened everywhere in the universe, which all emerged together from an expanding singularity. Thus, you and I are each standing at the center of this universe (but so is everybody and everything), a universe that is truly not big nor small nor great nor minute when human measure and relative self-comparisons are taken out of the equation.

The "whole universe in the ten directions" expresses the entirety of seamless space and time in which everything is connected to everything, and each point is one unique facet of everything else. Another friend, reflecting on the size of the universe relative to little planet Earth, professed that it made him feel small and insignificant. I told him that it should make him feel very big instead ... bigger and bigger each time he becomes aware of the expanding universe ... because it is all just him.

> It [the whole universe in the ten directions] is not vigorous like a fish jumping, nor revealed in perfectly still clarity. And because it is utterly beyond the coming and going of living and dying, it is coming and going, living and dying. Thus, because it is so, the past has gone from here, and the present comes from here.

Time is not only relative, but is also very much a human-made construct: time seems to have a before, a now, and an after. But is it possible to see the whole as just one moment ever unfolding? The past is simply now back then, now is now, and the future is a potential now to come. Zen masters of the past and present have said this. If time is just a measure of motion and change relative to location, then no time passes at the still center of the rotating hands of a clock. Some scientists say the same about the still center of black holes and other singularities from which moving universes may emerge and return. These are views of time (and timeless) freeing and very different from our ordinary human appraisal of time quickly passing, moving on to an uncertain future and our final oblivion in death.

And if the whole of the cosmos is still an expanding singularity much like a single pearl, what time is there and where is it but here and now wherever we look? The pearl is also a timeless and still singularity that gives rise to all the motion and passing time we now see. Likewise, the universe might be seen as a timeless and unmoved container for all the hustle and bustle of movement and flowing time within it. It is the hourglass that contains the sands of past becoming future. It is a still sea in which fish leap and swim, the open sky where birds fly, a blank sheet of paper on which all stories can be written. It is the still stage brought to life in dance. All events are moving time, yet timeless.

Yet, isn't the open sky still the same sky, with or without the vibrancy of the bird that comes to life within it? Isn't the pristine paper still paper no matter what words and pictures of life, love, and loss are written upon it? Is not the stage just as still and solid whatever show appears on it? Like the sky or the dance, life is coming and going in life and death, and yet is utterly beyond coming and going and life and death. The whole never departs from the whole. At the same time, one might say that the sky needs the bird to bring it to life, that paper is barren without stories, that the stage is unset until the vibrant dancing. Thus, from Dōgen in the "Genjō Kōan," "A bird flies through its sky, and no matter how far it flies, the sky is without end.... Thus we can conclude that ... air is life. The bird is life and ... life is the bird...."

This "utterly beyond the coming and going of living and dying" is the fertile foundation and source of all potentialities that arise and fade, appear and disappear, in this universe. It is an undivided whole that constantly manifests as all the myriad creatures and things, yet is always the undivided whole. When you see individuals, see the whole. When you see life and death, also see the birth and passing of the deathless. In counting time, feel the passing of the timeless.

Reality is thus both active and still, mysterious and quiet. It is this which Master Xuansha sings out as "the whole universe in the ten directions is one bright pearl." You, your life today, is also this fertile soil ready for the next planting and blossoming, a blank sheet ready for you to write upon, the stage for your dance.

When we are exploring the ultimate, who can see it utterly
as separate moments, bits and pieces? Who can truly speak
about it as but a total stillness?

In the ultimate, all time is swept into wholeness much as a single
water drop or ripple merges into the flowing sea. Fish also merge into
the waters, and birds into the sky. Actually, saying "merges" is not correct, for the drop or wave or fish or bird was never apart from the entire sea or sky, or the step from the dance. Dōgen thus reminds us to
know the separate as the whole, but also to know the whole as all the
separate things. The leaping fish is just the waters, but the waters are
leaping as the fish; the bird leaves no traces as it is the sky, while the
sky comes to life in the flight of the bird.

We do not need to ignore the separate to know the whole. Likewise, we can find all the motion and seeming confusion of this world
in the stillness and clarity that shines through, and know the stillness
and clarity as the motion and confusion in other guise.

"The whole universe in the ten directions" describes how
some endlessly chase things to make them benefit the self,
and some chase the self to make it comport with things.

As Master Dōgen points out many times in his writings, we try to
force this world into our self-created categories, the things we like and
the things we don't, and we impose all manner of other demands and
expectations upon people, things, and events. We create distance between the self and the world of apparently separate things by catego-
rizing and judging everything by our standards, and by wishing that it
all measure up to our mentally conceived ideals. The self becomes en-
slaved in suffering at the hands of its vision of the world. Further, we
think of our own self as another thing that we possess, imposing more
self-created categories on it, weighing its characteristics into aspects
we like and aspects we don't, and imposing all manner of other demands and expectations upon it. We try to pack the whole world into

little boxes of our liking, but nothing fits neatly into them, and we often encounter disappointment.

But when we allow the hard borders and frictions between ourself and the world to soften and fall, there is illumination. The people, things, and events of the world still won't be exactly as we might desire, yet we will feel the peace of allowing the world to just be the world. We can encounter this life and world as it is, on its own terms. We can let the things that we don't like—that sadden, or scare, or frustrate us—also be as they are.

Neither Buddha nor Dōgen can keep any of us from getting old and sick. However, their wisdom can show us how to accept our aging and frailty, and to flow with the passing years.

Dōgen went on to express it this way:

> It is said that when delusory emotion arises, division appears and wisdom is lost. This is to turn the head and change the face, to develop something and take advantage of an opportunity. Because we chase the self to make it comport with something, the whole of the ten directions is left in an endlessly restless state. Because the truth is forestalled, to experience the essential is beyond us.

The above is a somewhat obscure passage. Several respected translators disagree on the meaning of this section. However, I take it to mean that when we "chase things to make them benefit the self, and chase the self to make it comport with things," emotions arise and we experience a divided and restlessly non-stop world. This is why Dōgen wrote these two lines in the "Genjō Kōan":

> It is delusion to impose yourself and your desires upon life, demanding that the myriad things of the world be as you wish. To let the myriad things be as they are, illuminating yourself, is enlightenment.

In other words, when we try to get the world to conform to our desires, or force ourselves to fit circumstances, we do not accept and flow with things as they are.

To "turn the head and change the face" in modern Chinese is an idiom meaning to engage in false or superficial changes, whereby the true substance or reality remains hidden. We seek pleasing outcomes and run after opportunities and subjective ideals, remaining caught in surface appearances without seeing the underlying reality which transcends all that. There is a gap between self and life caused by our chasing after our desires. Because our hearts cannot rest in the world as it is, all is felt to be "left in an endlessly restless state." The truth of the flowing wholeness is hidden from our eyes, and the experience of peace is beyond us.

Duḥkha, the existential gap between how things are and how we wish them to be, is the reason we feel alienated from the circumstances of our lives, and therefore try desperately to fill that gap. The superficial changes we make, the things we buy to fill our closets, the trophies we rack up, the cosmetic efforts to keep a young appearance, are certainly "changing the head" but miss the true substance that is timeless. There is a gap between us and life, and our practice closes that gap:

> "The one pearl" is not its [actual] name but has come to be called such, and it nonetheless is a name that thoroughly expresses the truth. "The one pearl" must be the ten thousand years. When the onward stretching past has not yet departed, the onward stretching present is now arriving. The body is here now and the mind is here now, and this is the bright pearl. It is not just grass and trees here and there, nor mountains and rivers of heaven and earth, but it is the bright pearl.

This is another obscure passage that seems to mean that "one pearl" is not the real name of this world, yet somehow expresses its truth so well. Can we put a name on something which is everything? Call it Buddha or God or Dharmakāya or Universe or Reality or Everything and we still turn it into an idea. It's best not to apply any name to it. However, because we have to say something, this "one pearl" is not too bad an image to convey this unbroken wholeness.

The one pearl is all of passing time (the "ten thousand years") and it is also timeless. At the pivot point of it all, where past meets future, there is our body now and our mind now, all of which is the bright pearl. And whatever is the timeless aspect of reality, it is manifesting as and is part and parcel of this universe of time.

This reminds me of a famous Zen kōan that speaks of the "fiery *kalpa*," the eon of time in which the universe will end (rather than the cold finish that some scientists predict, but the point that the kōan makes is the same):

> A monk asked Master Dasui, "When the fire rages at the end of all eons and the whole universe is destroyed, is this destroyed or not?"
>
> Dasui responded, "Destroyed."
>
> The monk then said, "Then this goes along with that?"
>
> Dasui said, "This goes along with that."
>
> The monk asked Master Longji, "When the fire rages at the end of all eons and the whole universe is destroyed, is this destroyed or not?"
>
> Longji said, "Not destroyed."
>
> The monk said, "Why is this not destroyed?"
>
> Longji responded, "Because this is the same as the universe." (*Book of Serenity*, Case 30)

That which is timeless, which transcends all the individual things of the universe and passing time, is also manifesting and playing out as all those individual things and passing time. So, in one sense, when all the separate things and passing time come to an end, the timeless ends too. Where they go, the timeless goes. However, from another perspective, because that which is timeless and transcends all things is not just the things and passing time, it is *not* destroyed. We might say that, as the waves rise and fall, appear and vanish, it is the sea rising and falling, appearing and vanishing. Yet we can also say that the sea does not vanish with the wave. Thus, the vanishing is unvanishing, and the unvanishing is vanishing.

Likewise, the one pearl is not just the trees and mountains and other things of the world, for it is the bright pearl—a beautiful image of transcendence and immanence—yet it is also each and all of those things.

> [The student said to Xuansha], "How should I understand this [statement that the whole world is one pearl]?" Even though this seems to be a declaration of the monk's pleading ignorance and deluded karmic consciousness, it is also a clear manifestation of the great function right here. Stepping forward, one suddenly encounters that one foot of water is one foot of wave, that a yard of pearl is a yard of brightness. This is an expression of the truth passed from Buddha to Buddha, Ancestor to Ancestor, Xuansha to Xuansha.
>
> To voice this understanding, Xuansha responds, "The whole universe in the ten directions is one bright pearl. What use is understanding?" This expression is an expressing of the truth passed from Buddha to Buddha, Ancestor to Ancestor, Xuansha to Xuansha. If we wish to avoid this succession, perhaps we can do so for a time. Although we may avoid it for a while, any expression is just the time here and now of its manifesting.

Dōgen had a way of turning phrases such that a simple expression of ignorance becomes the whole universe functioning, the great activity, great dance. It shines through all things, even our momentary blindness and confusion.

When the monk says, "How should I understand [that the whole universe in the ten directions is one bright pearl]?" the question can be read a couple of ways. One is from the perspective of ignorance or, as Dōgen says, "deluded karmic consciousness," which means seeing things only in terms of subject and object, this and that, me and you. However, another way to understand this is through knowing that shines beyond subject and object, understanding or not understanding. It is like another famous kōan that describes the legendary meeting between Bodhidharma and Emperor Wu of China:

> "Who are you, standing in front of me?" asked the Emperor
> to Bodhidharma.
> "I don't know," said Bodhidharma.

We might take this to mean that Bodhidharma did not know who he was, or was just being evasive and teasing the Emperor. However, another way to understand this is that Bodhidharma knew well that there is no "I" to know and no separate object of knowing. Thus, Bodhidharma's statement really means "True knowing."

Of course, some not knowing is okay too. Despite a lifetime of Zen practice—and access to the best libraries and search engines on the planet—there are many facts about life and about ourselves that we may never know, and that is not a big problem. We may not know the name of the capital city of Brazil or how to fly a jet. We may not know how and why this world is as it is, who or what forces created it, or what the future holds. There are different kinds of knowledge. It is okay to not know everything.

That does not mean, however, that Zen practice cannot teach us much about who we are in the world. One fact that we can come to know firsthand through our Zen practice is that we are truly this world. About that fact there is no doubt, and "I don't know" means "knowing" when we drop from mind the "I" that feels like it stands separate from the world. In the above passage, Dōgen is playing with both meanings of not understanding or knowing.

The brightness shines in and through all facets of the pearl, large and small, beautiful or ugly, dark or light, understanding or deluded. Any one inch of this world is one inch of the whole pearl, just as any one inch of wave is one inch of sea. We can miss the fact for a time, be blind to it, but the truth is always present, manifesting right before our eyes and as our eyes themselves. When we realize it, it is passed from Buddha to Buddha, Ancestor to Ancestor, Xuansha to Xuansha, me to me, you to you, because all sense of separation among us drops away.

> At a later time, the master asked the same question of this monk, "The whole universe in the ten directions is one bright pearl, how do you understand this?" This is a statement that takes the prior day's statement and, adding a second layer, breathes it back today. Today he preaches it as something uncertain and indefinite. Pushing over yesterday's words, he is nodding and laughing. The monk asks, "The whole universe in the ten directions is one bright pearl. What use is understanding?" We might tell him, "This is just the robber riding the robber's horse to chase the robber. An ancient Buddha, preaching to you, goes among the varied kinds of beings." Now, turn the light inward and illuminate for a time. How many are there of this "What use is understanding?" You might say, "Seven milk cakes and five herb cakes," or that "There is preaching south of the River Xiang and north of the River Tan."

I take the opening of this passage to mean that Dōgen turned around the monk's original question, "How do you understand?" to bring out fresh insights. Dōgen often uses "how" and "what" and other interrogatives not to actually question, but as vibrant declarations for the whole of creation, the great function, the great activity. "How?" becomes "How!" as in a joyous "How about that!" or "That's how!" "What?" in Dōgen's hands becomes *"What!"* as in "That's what's what!" or "What a lark!" If you fail to get this declaration of *How! What!* then you are like the robber chasing the robber on the robber's own horse—just a dog chasing its own tail, which is already present all along.

Dōgen says that the Buddha travels all over, preaching his message to all kinds of ears. Can you hear it? Sit zazen and turn on the light of silence and still clarity within. A poem by the great Zen master Shitou Xiqian describes zazen this way: "Turn around the light to shine within, and just return. The vast inconceivable source cannot be faced nor turned away from." Turning the light around, all separation and friction drop away. All the seemingly varied things of this world—all the differently flavored cakes Dōgen mentions—are six of one, half a dozen of another, made of the same flour heated in the same oven though producing differing tastes. Then, whether north or south of the rivers Xiang and Tan—or any river—it is here, there, and everywhere, right here and nowhere at all. You and all things are in just the right place. Nonetheless, if we hold this as only an intellectual idea, old Xuansha will pull the rug out from under us, as he did this monk, until we truly understand.

But then Dōgen takes it even a step further, leaping beyond with a bit of his trademark word-jazz, to demonstrate that both ignorance and understanding, all cakes both bitter and sweet, every drop of one river and all rivers, wet or dry, are the one pearl:

> Xuansha responded, "I see that you are making a livelihood inside the demon's cave on the black mountain." Know that the sun face and moon face have not changed places since ages past. The sun's face emerges together with the sun's face, the moon's face emerges together with the moon's face. Thus, it was said [quoting master Yaoshan Weiyan], "Even if I say that it is the sixth month, the hottest time of the summer, it is not possible to say that my nature is hot." Thus, this timeless bright pearl is boundless, and all the universe in all directions is one bright

pearl, not two pearls or three. The entire body is but one
true Dharma eye, the entire body is the true substance,
the entire body is a single phrase. The entire body is
brightness, the entirety of body is the entirety of mind.
When the entirety of body is the entirety of body, there
are no hindrances. It is perfectly round, and roundly rolls
round and round.

Dōgen brings light into the usually dark connotations of the phrase
about making a living in the "demon's cave on the black mountain."
In Zen parlance, it is usually taken to mean that a practitioner is lost
in intellectual ideas or dull blankness. Instead, Dōgen sees beyond the
darkness of the cave. He offers images of the sun and moon, day and
night, light and dark, hot and cold, good and bad. He notes that all
arise together, for they are all just the one bright pearl.

The sun and moon do not actually change places, for when one
emerges the other is also present. Whether in the heat of summer or
the dead of winter, the true nature is beyond hot or cold and all passing seasons. (My friend in Australia likes to remind me that the "sixth
month" is the dead of winter there!)

The one bright pearl is all things, all names and words. At the same
time, it is the one truth, the one substance, the word of words, the
total brightness, the entire body, the entire mind. Thus, the whole
universe and all it contains rolls on and on without hindrance.

Because the power of the bright pearl manifests in realization like this, there are Avalokiteśvaras and Maitreyas in
the present, seeing form and hearing sounds. Old and new
Buddhas manifest their bodies and preach the Dharma
teachings.

When we understand this one bright pearl, all the bodhisattvas
and every Buddha is right here, preaching and teaching. Master Shitou also declares in his famous ode describing his home and his life in

a little grass hut on a mountain: "Will this hut perish or not? Perishing or not, the original master is present, not dwelling south or north, east or west. [ . . . ] Meet the ancestral teachers, be familiar with their instructions [ . . . ] If you want to know the undying person in the hut, don't separate from this skin bag here and now."[4]

If you wish to meet all the Buddhas, Great Bodhisattvas, and Ancestors (such as Avalokiteśvara, who represents compassion, and Maitreya, the future Buddha), just sit zazen in this skin bag of yours—in your own body with all its wrinkles and blemishes. Then, as Shitou enjoins us, "Turn around the light to shine within, and just return. The vast inconceivable source cannot be faced nor turned away from." At that point, all the buddhas, bodhisattvas, and ancestors come alive in your very sitting.

> Just at this present moment, the bright pearl hangs suspended in space, is sewn into your robe, is kept under a dragon's chin or tied in a topknot. This one bright pearl is so and thus is the entire universe in the ten directions. If to be sewn inside a robe is its situation, do not try to hang it outside the robe. If to be tied inside a topknot or held under a chin is its situation, do not try to play with it outside the topknot or chin.

Dōgen refers to several well-known stories. The black dragon guards the pearl of truth under her chin. The *Lotus Sutra* contains a parable of a king who keeps a precious pearl in his topknot, sharing it only when the time is right. They have this treasure but do not easily share it. Another parable tells of the friend of a drunken man who sews a pearl into the latter man's robe. The drunken man is unaware of the pearl and does not learn that it's in his possession until much later. This last story represents an individual who possesses a treasure, yet is unaware of it. Ignorance hides it from his eyes, just as we do not realize we are the one bright pearl that is always ours.

Dōgen then goes on to imply that all the pearls are in their rightful places, hidden or not. The pearl is still the pearl whether hidden or not. He seems to mean that all this world is the pearl always in its rightful place, and we should know this fact even when not yet clearly seen. One cannot bring out the pearl from where it rests, for there is no inside or outside that is not already the one pearl. Nonetheless, let us each do our best to bring forth and show the pearl that is our birthright, and not keep it hidden from view.

> When we are drunk, there are close friends who sew a pearl inside our clothes, and we should always give a pearl to a close friend. When a pearl is given to us, we are always intoxicated.

Dōgen takes the *Lotus Sutra* parable and reenvisions the sequential story (a man sews a pearl into the clothes of a friend who later finds it). Instead, Dōgen bends time and cause-effect into an image of flowing interconnection and relationship. We now give the pearl to the friend. Everything is the pearl—you, the friend, and sewing. The intoxication is not limited to place and time, for the pearl is boundless and the drunkenness is itself the boundless pearl. The same is true of friends and friendship, and the giving that always happens without measure of time. It is all one bright pearl.

> That which is already truly such is the one bright pearl that is the universe in the ten directions. So, even though it seems to be continuously changing in outward appearance, such is just the bright pearl. The very knowing that the pearl is indeed such, this too is just the bright pearl. The bright pearl's infinite colors and forms are encountered in this way.

Nothing escapes this bright pearl, for even this knowing and pondering about the bright pearl is the bright pearl.

Because all is already truly thus, those who doubt and think "I am not the pearl" should not doubt that they are the pearl. Whether you doubt or not, such doubt and thinking, accepting, or rejecting are all just small views. This is nothing more than trying to fathom and squeeze these views into your narrow intellect.

We are the wholeness whether we doubt it or not, feel it or not. Further, any attempt to name or define the wholeness has to be something of a failure in the end. Better to just realize it.

How could we not cherish the bright pearl? Its radiant colors and brilliance are endless. Each one color and all drops of light and every ray of light at each moment and in every circumstance in all its variegations are the virtue of the whole universe in the ten directions. No one can snatch that away. No one can toss it like a shard of tile into a street market. Do not worry whether or not you will fall into the chain of karmic causality to be reborn into the six states [the six possible kinds of rebirth, with heavens and hells and humans in between]. They are each and all the never obscured original state from first to last, and the pearl is the face and the eye.

This everything that is everything is all things in all their permutations. Thus, the pearl cannot be taken or tossed away like a broken tile in the gutter. It sweeps in and leaps beyond the question of rebirth in traditional Buddhism, for reborn or not, all is the one pearl beyond birth and death from the start. All such things are thoroughly the pearl, and our face and eyes are the face and eyes of the pearl too.

Yet neither you nor I truly know what the bright pearl is and is not, have hundreds of thoughts and hundreds of negations of thought about what it is and is not, which form into fixed and positive notions. At the same time, by virtue of Xuansha's words of the Dharma, we realize that from the very first our own bodies and minds have already been the bright pearl, and that therefore the mind is not the self. So why be attached to whether it is a bright pearl or not a bright pearl, whether birth and death are the bright pearl? Even if we are perplexed and anxious, this is no different from the bright pearl. There has never been any action or thought produced by something that is not the bright pearl. Therefore, our every step, forward or backward in the demon's cave of the black mountain, is simply one bright pearl.

Dōgen closes with a reminder that this wholeness and reality is what it is, whether we truly understand it or have wrong or partial ideas about it. It does not matter what we call it, if we choose to call it. Nonetheless, we realize that this is who we are, and so our minds are not only the self, for they are ultimately the pearl. Our very perplexity is the pearl. Our every thought and act is the pearl. Of course, the sitting of zazen is the bright pearl sitting perfectly as the bright pearl. Our stubbed toes or any other crisis in life are the bright pearl.

Dōgen first wrote these words in 1238, in Kyoto, Japan. That time and place was the time and place of the one bright pearl, and now is the time and here is the place of the one bright pearl. All of life, the great and the narrow, happy or sad, sick or healthy, up or down, near and far, sweet or sour, beautiful and ugly, living or dead—the one bright pearl which is all that and shines through it. This pearl has been sewn in your robes all along.

I bet you never knew that you were so wealthy.

# Being-Time

It has been some months since my surgery and the doctors say that they got the cancer. They say I should see many more birthdays, assuming I don't get hit by a bus or encounter something else along the way.

One of my Japanese doctors turned out to be a zazen practitioner with an interest in Dōgen. I am glad that he got off his cushion long enough to master that procedure and understood that "nothing to attain" did not prevent him from becoming an excellent surgeon.

This experience did add a few more scars to my body and wrinkles to my face. But perhaps these are due to the normal passage of time. The thought sometimes crosses my mind—as it does for anyone else— that the years are flying by, and I wonder where they've gone. It seems that I was just a little kid, then a teenager, and now I see white hairs and my father's face looking at me in the mirror. When I sit zazen, my knees ache some days. How much more sand is left in my personal hourglass?

Fortunately, Dōgen left us with an interpenetrating vision of time, inspired by the Huayan and other Mahayana masters, as well as his

117

own insight. Hundreds of years before Einstein made "relative time" a household world, Dōgen spoke of each of us, and all things, existing in our own vibrant being-time, connected to the being-time of all other beings and things in this vast, fluid universe.

Why is this important? Because it allows us to see the amazing, syncopated, backward-forward, moving-still, timeless-time of the great dance. It also frees us from simply witnessing time as an unstoppable flood in which our youth turns to old age, time passes quickly, life becomes death, and all is nothing but change. The Buddha taught that all composite things are impermanent and ever changing, but he also taught a way beyond all things and change.

Dōgen also knew this way of experiencing time that goes beyond time and no time, where all of time is held in each moment. Actually, we might better speak of ways (plural) of experiencing times and time-less. Dōgen lived an interflowing time and being, knew time as being, *your* being-time, which is a moment of the being-time of all the world.

Happy Non-Birthday! Birth and passing time are not all there is.

Happy Now-Birthday, now and now and now! In each and every moment, you and all the world are reborn.

Happy All-Birthday! As future flows into the past and present, while past becomes the future and present, we become younger and older and just this present age at once. One might say that this present instant holds fully your infancy and dotage, not to mention every moment from Big Bang to the universe's Big Finale.

And on and on . . .

If you doubt the utility of Dōgen's words, please hear them as medicine for our human tendency to experience time as a one-way rush from birth to death, bound in between by clock and calendar. Our time of life is timeless too, as is each moment in it. Dōgen speaks with images meant to show our intimate identity with this universe and all things in it, whether existing for just an instant, billions of years, or endless ages, time long or short.

I am going to be a little freer and "revision-ing" in my expression of what Dōgen said in his *Shōbōgenzō* "Uji" (Being-Time). I want to convey the timeless meaning of the old master's words in a way that makes sense for modern times, but I will also try to stay close to his original wording as much as possible. If you can, please compare my interpretation with any of the excellent English translations now available.

I advise you to take your time with this piece. Read little bits, then put it down for a while. Savor each section in its own time, letting it work on you. You might even want to read this text back to front, or jump around in place and time. You might want to savor each word or each part of a word, both of which encompass the whole piece. That's much like Dōgen's sense of time(s) which stop, start, flow back and forth, are one moment, all moments, and so on. Any way you want to read, I thank you in advance for your time.

> An old master named Yaoshan said:
>> For the time being standing on top of the highest peak, just being-time.
>> For the time being moving along the bottom of the deepest sea, being-time.
>> For the time being the three heads and eight arms of a fighting demon, being-time.
>> For the time being the eight- or sixteen-foot body of a golden Buddha, being-time.
>> For the time being this staff or whisk here held, being-time.
>> For the time being a pillar or lantern, being-time.
>> For the time being the children of common families like the Zhang and the Li, being-time.
>> For the time being the earth and sky, being-time.
>> In this word "being-time," time is already just being, and all being is time.

By quoting Yaoshan, Dōgen starts off explaining that being and time are one, that being-time is everything, and that each place and thing and moment is also its own being-time. There isn't anything in this great world that is not the acting of time, no moment in this boundless universe that is not the flowing of being. Yaoshan said it is so from the highest peak to the lowest point of the sea, from earth to sky, for you and me and all the things to be found, for the enlightened and the unenlightened, for statues of golden Buddhas of any size, and for demons too. It is so for all things, all people whatever their name, all places on earth or in space. Each and all are being-time, and all together are the great being-time.

But what exactly does Dōgen mean when he says that "time is already just being, and all being is time"?

If I had to put it simply, I might say that the existence of all things—even those we might consider lifeless—is their own individual being, which is also their own individual making of time. You have your being which is your time, and I have my being which is my time. We might almost say that you are a universe of one, all your own and measured by its own clocks, but likewise for every other thing or being, each in their own universe with their own times, and all our universes interflow and interact. Seven centuries after Dōgen, Einstein confirmed that time is relative by showing that it passes more slowly for a twin on top of a mountain—who is thus farther away from the gravitational pull of Earth's mass—than for his brother in a valley.

This moment of time is my time for being, as is your moment of time for being. What is more, all our times interconnect with and interflow into each other, are long or short or beyond measure, depending on how we look at things. Time moves beyond me and you and other things too, and flows in all kinds of directions besides the conventional past to future. This is what Master Dōgen describes.

It's quite a lively vision of time!

The sixteen-foot golden Buddha body is time itself too. Because it is time, it shines forth with the resplendent illumination of time. We should learn this in the ordinary twenty-four hours of today. The three heads and eight arms of a demon are also time itself. Because they are the same, they are just the same time as the twenty-four hours of today. We really cannot measure how long or far away, or how short and pressing, are twenty-four hours.

All our ordinary measures of good and bad, derived from the wisdom of Buddhas or the ignorance of fighting demons, are the universe's being-time, as well as our personal being-time, in each and all of the twenty-four hours. Your doing of evil is a moment of evil being-time, and likewise for a moment of good being-time.

The "eight- or sixteen-foot" golden Buddha refers to either a sitting or a standing Buddha. But it is also an encouragement to find wisdom in all aspects of our lives, whether we're sitting or standing, walking or being still. As for the three heads and eight arms of a fighting demon, in Buddhist art both Buddhas and demons are typically depicted in many forms, some of them having several heads and arms.

However, there is also a way to know a peaceful and whole reality beyond good and bad, big or small, moving or sitting still. While each has its own unique and complete moment of time by one perspective, and while the day is twenty-four hours and the joining of all moments together, in the wisdom of a Buddha, time is also seen as timeless and fluid beyond all measure. Thus each moment is itself, is all of the twenty-four hours and all times of the universe, yet is not those measures too.

The way that time seems to flow, coming and departing, seems clear, so people do not doubt it. They do not doubt it, but that does not mean that they truly know it. Even doubt is flowing time, such that even the doubts that living beings hold about every thing and every fact that we do not know are always different and changing with time. Our past doubts are not always the same as our presently held doubts. Nonetheless, each such doubt itself is nothing other than time.

We have had doubts and worries about the future in the past. We may have doubts today and other doubts tomorrow. Right now, reading this, you may be starting to have doubts about the solidity of time, doubts that did not exist minutes ago. Even doubts change with time, like all things. In fact, even the changing doubt is each and all your being-time, each its own moment of believing or doubting.

> The manner the self arrays itself is itself the form of the entire world, every state of the self is a showing of the whole universe. Thus, each individual being and each object of this whole world must be seen as individual moments of time. Therefore the things of the world stand unimpeded and unhindering in relation to all, in the same way that moments of time do not hinder other moments of time.

Every person, thing, and event is an expression of time and being in that moment and place of time. Each might be thought of as its own complete moment of time in that place and moment. We can learn to see each and all, unimpeded and unhindering of all the rest of the world, just as two seconds of flowing time stand each on their own, undisturbed, and do not interfere with the flowing of each other. This moment is thoroughly this moment, whole and complete, and this is so for the next moment, and the moment after that.

It is lovely to learn to experience each moment and event in life as whole and complete unto itself; even the moments that do not always please us. This moment is just this moment, and that event is just that event. Likewise, this thing is just this thing that is what it is, and that thing is just that thing, whole and unimpeded like its own island of being and time. So it is for all the people, places, things, and events of life. Most personally, I put this to work in my bed in the cancer ward, opening my mind to experience the time of sickness as just that time of sickness, not to be rejected nor compared to any times of health. Of course, that did not prevent me from also spending my time (another simultaneous time I had) to seek health, working to recover and heal.

For this reason, the mind that first seeks to pursue the [Buddha] Way is arising in this moment. A way-seeking moment arises in this mind. It is the same with practice and attaining the way. [The mind that practices in this moment is the moment that practices in this mind. The mind that attains in this moment is the attaining moment in this mind]. Thus, the self that acts and arrays itself sees itself as time itself. This is the expression of the self that is time.

We know, in one way to view time, that Buddhist practice appears to take many years, perhaps whole lifetimes, as we progress from beginner to master to Buddha somewhere down the line. Yet Dōgen paints a picture where all is just this very moment of time. Our thoughts, actions, and the flowing world are so connected in each moment that each moment is the flowing of our thoughts and actions and the whole world.

What is more, a thing or person not only has its flowing being-time, but being-time has its flowing thing or person. Thus, the mind that attains enlightenment in a moment is, no less, the moment that attains enlightenment as the mind. Bringing it down to earth, the mind that scrubs a dish in a moment of time is a moment of being and time scrubbing a dish. It is a dish scrubbing time, and a scrub dishing time. You are time, the scrubbing is time, as is the dish, the cleaning and the grime are just time, and time is just the grime scrub-dishing you, dish you-griming scrub, and so on. All of life is so.

But what's the use of all this? It sounds a bit crazy.

It is good to know that each moment of our lives is the life of the universe, the universe come to life, and that the times of our lives are the lives and times of all reality. You think that it is just you sitting zazen for a while, or even washing a dish or walking the dog for a few minutes. Do you also get a sense that you, and what you do, are much more than that? Can you feel the whole world and all time flowing in and out of what you do? From the time you first thought about practicing Buddhism until becoming a Buddha; from the first instant of taking up a dirty dish in your humble kitchen until it is scrubbed and on the shelf; both before, during, and after the time that your being-time and the dog's being-time momentarily intersect—all of these are the ongoing dance of the whole world's time, dancing as your movements and being, all in partnership with everything else.

And you thought that washing the supper dishes was just washing the supper dishes, that dog walking was taking up your precious time!

> We should come to know in this way that there are myri-
> ads of forms of things, hundreds of blades of grasses
> through the earth, and that each blade of grass and each
> single appearance is not apart from the entire earth. Hold-
> ing this view is the starting point of practice. And when
> we arrive in the field of the ineffable, there is not but one
> blade of grass and one appearance here and now. Whether
> there is understanding of this phenomenon or no under-
> standing of this phenomenon, whether there is under-
> standing of things or no understanding of things, all is
> only this exact moment. Since there is nothing but just
> this moment, the time-being is all the time there is. All
> moments of being-time are just the whole of time, as all
> existent things are time too. The whole universe exists in
> individual moments of time, and each moment contains
> all existences and all worlds. Reflect now whether any
> being or any world or the whole universe is left out of the
> present moment of time.

No being, no thing, no grain of sand nor planet, no galaxy nor the whole universe is apart from this present moment of time. And all moments of time, whether the past or future, are just this present moment of time, for this present moment of time is just this present moment of time as it was or as it will be. However, in reality there is no single "moment of time," for my time is not your time or anything else's. Each exists in its own time.

Likewise, all things and beings of this earth are just this earth, and all moments of this earth, whether past or future, are just this present earth both then and as it will be. This is so for all things in the universe and all things of your life. All moments, past or future, fully hold and are all other moments. What is more, the time of all beings and things, grains of sand, and planets, this world or any other, or even whole universes, are just your time, and your being is theirs as well. Nonetheless, their time is just their time, and not yours at all.

Even if you cannot get your head around all these time(s) standing still and apart or flowing and merging, all as one and one in all, get on the zazen sitting cushion for a time and just feel this interflowing in all directions.

So, as you celebrate another birthday, know that the burning candles on the cake are just the earth itself come alight. All of time is one burning flame that burns in the past, present, and future, yet remains the one flame burning. Nonetheless, this moment of burning is only this moment of the candle burning, with no before or after, and nothing else in the world. Thus this one moment of burning is all the burning that ever was or will be. Each moment of candle burning is all the things and events of the universe burning, and there is nothing apart. So blow out that candle which cannot be extinguished. Your own life can also never be extinguished even when, someday, your own flame burns out. What more could you possibly wish for?

Whether we are just beginning practice or have thoroughly mastered it, see or cannot see, know or do not know, makes no difference. Knowing or not knowing, beginning or mastering, is just this one present moment, which is the time-being of all there is. Each moment of being-time is all of time known as all phenomena, all existences, and all worlds. If Buddha is timeless, then becoming Buddha is just this time and all moments too. All of it is your time.

This is not an experience of time that an ordinary timepiece can capture.

> Yet, common people who do not understand Buddha-dharma, the Buddha's truth, may think the following when they hear about "being-time": "I suppose that there are times when I am being like an angry demon with three heads and eight arms, and there are times when I am being like a tall, golden Buddha. When I cross a river or cross a mountain, after I have crossed them, they may still exist, but I have moved on and they are in my past. Now perhaps I have arrived at some great, high red-towered palace far distant, and the mountains and rivers are as far from me as heaven is from earth."

Ordinary people think only of past, present, and future, time moving on, and the distance between what is and what was or will be. We have either moved on or have not yet arrived. Perhaps we think of enlightenment as a great palace that we'll reach after a long trip through the mountains, and thus fail to experience the great palace that is in each step all along this plain earth.

> But time is not merely this, nor just a single line. That is to say, when I was climbing the mountain or crossing the river, I was there in that time. As I was present, time was me. And I actually exist now, so time has not departed. If time is not marked by coming and going, the time of climbing the mountain is the present of being-time. If time does take the form of coming and going, one still has this present moment of being-time which is just being-time itself. Thus, how could the time of climbing the mountain and the time of crossing the river fail to fully swallow and spit out this time now in the red-towered palace?

Dōgen's vision of time might become clearer if we envision our-selves in the present moment, standing on top of the highest cliff in which the past and future stretch unimpeded beyond the farthest horizon. Picture the whole scene, horizon to horizon, as a single panorama of being-time. It is one moment that actually includes your past and your future simultaneously, yet can all be taken in as one moment.

Or picture time as a single ocean that is the same ocean no matter where on its surface a vessel rests. Then, wherever the vessel moves is still the one moment of oceanic time. Or perhaps it is like a music re-cord that contains the entire song of your life or all of history, begin-ning, middle, and end. Whatever is played on that record, wherever the needle is dropped, is the one record of being-time.

In that sense, time held within the record or sea never comes and goes even as it appears to come and go. What is more, the past, pres-ent, and future all sail the same one ocean, flow over the same moun-tain range, or play the same beautiful song. Thus our being swallows up and breathes out the time before approaching the mountains and the time of each step climbing the mountains—both are the moun-taintop and the valley. The towering red palace of enlightenment is now fully held in every winding step up the mountain of life, or whether sailing its oceans and crossing its streams.

Leaving oceans and music, mountains, rivers, and red towers aside, it is just your day-to-day life. If you nursed a sick child years ago, this is not really a past event, for all is this same one moment of time; your first or sixteenth birthday is fully contained in your fiftieth or eighti-eth. The flame of being-time burns brightly right now. Each moment of your life was just the one moment of your life that is the same right then and right now, which also is the same one moment of all time in the universe. And each of the single moments of your life swallows up and burns with all the other single moments.

It is so for all the good and bad days, angry and peaceful days of life, as Dōgen now describes:

Three heads and eight arms [of the angry demon] may be yesterday's time. The eight- or sixteen-foot body [of a golden Buddha] may be today's time. But what we call yesterday and today are actually just one time in which we go directly into the mountains and look across thousands or tens of thousands of peaks at a glance. Time itself does not flow [even as it flows in our experience], yesterday's and today's time do not go away from such a vantage point. The moment of yesterday's angry demon passes instantly as this being-time. Though it seems to be now distant, it is just moments of the present. It looks like it is over there, but it is now. The moment of today's golden Buddha also passes instantly as this being-time. Though it seems to be nearby, it is also just moments of the present. It looks like it is here or there, but it is now.

The bad of the past is gone, yet is still here within the sweep of the panorama. Goodness may be present today, and enlightenment may seem in the distant future, yet all is still just here. It is as if for Dōgen the entire history of the universe, from its earliest moment until its end, is like a story being told on a single page—all past events and possible future events are each contained on the single page that is right here, right now, manifesting as our present life and all our lives of this single being-time. A pen is in our hands and—while we share the role of author with our fellow sentient beings and all the world— what we do with that pen determines so much. Will we help write stories of angry demons, or of peace and goodness like a Buddha?

I feel that Master Dōgen would want to leave with us the sense that our present moment and all that happened in our lives in the past for good and bad, and all that may happen in the future, and all that is happening across the world, and all that happened or may happen billions of years from now across the galaxy—all these are one thing. All are flowing in and through you. That's what he wished to do with the words he offered and which are heard by you right now and will still resonate tomorrow.

This being so, each pine tree is time, each bamboo is time.

Every tree or bamboo or grain of sand of the entire being-time mountain range is being and time. Every drop and square inch of the being-time ocean is being and time. Every step of the being-time dance of the universe is being and time. Every word on the page is being-time. Every dish washed, every sick child nursed, all trips to the office or cemetery, just being-time being-time. Nothing is left out.

So, we should not understand only that time flies by. We should not feel that "flying" is time's only ability. For if we just let time fly away, separations from and in it might appear. Those who fail to experience and grasp the truth of being-time do so because they only understand time as something that passes.

Ultimately all existences are linked and become time. Everything that exists throughout the whole universe is lined up in a series of all individual moments, and at the same time is each and all time. Because all moments are being-time [and you are being-time], they are your being-time.

And because time has the nature of flowing, today flows into tomorrow while today flows into yesterday, all as yesterday flows into today, today flows into today, and tomorrow flows into tomorrow.

Picture this as tracing recorded data on an electronic disk front to back or back to front. It is not that Dōgen was a rigid determinist, feeling that all the data on the disk is prewritten and not subject to change. Far from it. His view of karma and the good or bad effects that result from our present and past actions allowed for endless opportunities for choice in the pivot point of the present—just like a disk containing a game with a range of prewritten possibilities relies on the player's choices, good and bad, here and now.

Being-time has the quality of passing in a series of moments too. "Today" passes through a series of moments from today to tomorrow, and from today through a series of moments to yesterday. From yesterday, it passes through a series of moments to today. And from tomorrow, it passes through a series of moments to further tomorrows.

From our bird's-eye vantage point, we can witness time as something more than merely past becoming present, then charging forward into the future. We might instead see time as the whole electronic disk, which seems to have events of the past firmly recorded, events of the present being inscribed now, and events of the future still open space and undetermined. However, looking panoramically, we see all as the single disk, in which the parts of the disk holding the past, the present, and space for the open future depend on each other. To maintain the wholeness and integrity of the disk with no parts missing, past needs present and space for the future, the still open sectors of future need both past and present to determine them, and present needs future and past if it is not to simply stand still. You cannot have past without future and present, nor future without present and past, and present would be frozen in place without the other two. It is much like saying that, if time is like a river, there can be no downstream without the upstream, nor upstream without a downstream, yet all is the one river flowing. It is so even though the waters upstream have not yet reached downstream, much as time has not yet reached and settled the future. Still, upstream depends on the downstream space into which to flow, and downstream is useless without an upstream to send it waters.

Time's arrow seems only to fly in one direction, from past to future. However, theoretically, it need not be so. If time is like a river or disk, downstream also flows into upstream if we reverse the current, or play the disk in reverse. Modern physics has come intriguingly close to this by saying that all timelines actually can be seen as potentially running in two directions (the dominoes falling down can also be seen as the dominos unfalling up), even though we only experience time's arrow moving one way. Only entropy causes us to keep moving forward in time and not backward.

Even if we see this in simpler terms, it is not so hard to understand that the future affects the past. If some terrible event happened in the past, it might seem as if that history was written in stone and beyond change. In one sense, this is true. However, in another sense, the past just exists as a present memory of the mind, and the future is filled with open possibilities. How we think and choose to handle a remembered event can change the past.

For example, if I choose to forgive or not forgive a past wrong, the memory of the event—which is most of what remains—is changed. If in the future I choose to make up for my mistake, perhaps by seeing that it doesn't repeat, I can change the meaning of the past in that way too. If my friend did some hurtful act to me many years ago, events really never existed for me apart from my view and feelings about the act that I witnessed. That view then became a memory and continuing feelings, all that remains of the past act. If today, years later, I gain new information about why my friend acted that way, or otherwise let my grudge go, I am truly rewriting history and my view of what transpired. Since my view and feelings were all that I ever had about the act to start with, we might say that the past is changed. Further, our memories of the past are always incomplete. We have limited and subjective views, we drop and add facts and interpretations as the years pass, sometimes recalling details which are pure imagination. Truly, the past is constantly changing.

I have had such conversations with some of my students, victims of violence years ago, who can either choose to keep the past alive or let it go in their current thinking. (I usually advise them to remember and learn from the event, recognizing the scars, recognizing their possible anger, yet to let it go too. In our Zen way of seeing and experiencing things many ways at once, we have the power to recall and let go at the same time. Do not forget, accept that you are a human being feeling pain, yet release the past in some way too.) Also, their future actions from now on—to ensure that the violence does not repeat into future generations—can affect the past in that way too, such that the past does not repeat.

Dōgen next reminds us how wonderful it is that time flows at all:

> And because flowing is a quality of time, moments of past
> and present do not pile up on top of one another or line up
> in a row.

Time flows and changes, yet is also timeless when seen as a whole. Because the whole is flowing, it is alive and not frozen. Moments do not crash into each other or gum up the works. Each moment has its place and time; nevertheless, the whole mountain range, ocean, disk, river, or dance is timeless, containing each and all as one, even as it keeps on flowing and moving.

If time did not flow, and life did not move, we would be as if trapped in ice or stone. We should be grateful that time flows, and that things move on, and that they don't get stuck or pile up on each other. In fact, the world would not turn, life would not develop, children would not be born, without flowing time.

You and I may be getting older because of time's flowing, but be grateful, for otherwise there would be no life to live.

> Because there is no piling up or congestion, the times of
> each of the Zen Ancestors of the past was their time. Mas-
> ter Zhigong is time in his time; Master Huangbo is time
> in his time; Master Mazu is time in his time; Master Shi-
> tou is time in his time. Because self and not the self, self
> and others are just already one time, this very moment of
> practice-enlightenment is time.

This very moment of your practice is the time of all the practice of all the masters of the past, and is all time practicing in this very moment. Our realization about practice is practice-enlightenment. Each master sat zazen in his or her own time, yet your time of sitting zazen is nothing but the time of their sitting and the whole world's sitting as one time.

> Our ordinary daily struggles, like getting splattered with mud or splashed with water, are also time. But the views of the common person, and what they see as the causal relations of things and events, are not really the true reality. The reality is that the workings of the laws of causes and conditions put ordinary people into temporary causal relations for the time being. But because they understand this time and this existence to be other than reality itself, they believe that the sixteen-foot golden body of Buddha is far removed. They try to ignore and evade the fact that they are the sixteen-foot golden body of Buddha, thinking "I am not that." But even in such a case, all that is just bits and pieces of being-time. Please explore this fact deeply.

We consider Buddha as distant because we fail to know the mountain range or dance in which all is all, each is each, each is each other, and each is all. Therefore, something seems distant when all is present here, right in this muddy world of daily struggles. Of course, just because Buddha and each and all of us are one, if we do not manifest this truth with our actions, words, and thoughts, but instead act like an angry demon or a fool, then Buddha is here (and is each of us) but not manifest. Just because we already are this dance of the universe, that is no excuse to not dance gracefully.

> Being-time also causes noon and two o'clock to be arranged as they are in the world today, for each is a rising and falling

of the being-time ineffably abiding in its place in each moment. Midnight is time and four in the morning is time. Living beings are time and Buddhas are time. This time sometimes experiences the whole universe using the three heads and eight arms [of the evil demon] and sometimes experiences the whole universe using a sixteen-foot golden Buddha body. To universally actualize the whole universe by using the whole universe is "to perfectly actualize." Thereby, to fully actualize the golden body of Buddha by using the golden body of a Buddha—to first arouse the way-seeking mind, to practice, to attain enlightenment, and then enter [final] nirvana—is entirely nothing but being itself, is nothing but time itself. It is only the perfect realization and actualization of the whole of time as all being. There is nothing remaining to be left out.

All is being-time, all is Buddha, whatever time of day, and is so even if we hide the fact by acting instead with the ignorance and narrow vision of an evil demon. The entire path of a Buddhist student, from the first calling to walk the way through practice, attaining realization, and finally dying and returning to that which has never truly been left, is all Buddha actualizing Buddha by searching for Buddha and living like Buddha would. The universe is fully actualized by how we, its players, actualize our lives. Thus, make Buddha real in this world by acting like Buddha (avoid being a demon). All of it is the full catastrophe, the whole works—all are totally being-time, no matter what happens.

Because something left over is just something left over, even a moment of delusion or only half-understood being-time is the perfect realization of delusion and half of being-time fully understood. Even heedlessly mistaken views and descriptions are also being-time. If we leave it utterly up to being, even the moments before and the moments after the heedless mistake each abide in their own place in being-time. Each is abiding in its own place in the Dharma as a state of vigorous activity in each moment which is just being-time.

Dōgen envisions this being-time as whole and complete even when, in our delusion, we fail to recognize it as such. Nonetheless, our failure itself—which divides up time into discreet moments and alienates us from them—is nonetheless a whole and complete failure that is perfect in its instant of failure. Even our moments in life of falling on our ass are perfectly ass falling. They too are being-time. (Nonetheless, we should try to avoid such falling, for not falling is also being-time.) Dōgen describes each moment and event as abiding in its own place. All is being-time, whether or not this moment of being-time consists of our being too foolish to know this.

I believe it is a great misconception to think that someone who has mastered Zen—if mastery is possible—is always supposed to be as perfect as a golden Buddha, beyond all error and mistake, bad hair day or failing. This is an image painted in our legends and stories in which the hero or religious saint is always perfect. Dōgen, as I read him, was a man of great wisdom, but also had human quirks. In a few of his writings, he can seem a bit short tempered sometimes, or disappointed at events, like any of us. He called monks he disapproved of "sons of the devil," bald-headed non-humans who are "dumber than beasts."[5] It is said that Dōgen once tossed a monk out of the monastery for failing to follow instructions, even having the dirt below the place where the man sat dug up! I don't believe that either Dōgen or the Buddha were always feeling at one with the universe, always doing what needed to be done in every situation, always speaking with a Buddha's tongue.

Many Buddhists will chastise me for my more fallible picture of a flesh-and-blood Buddha. But in my view, a Buddha is a Buddha in those moments of being-time when they are acting like a Buddha and in those moments of being-time when they fail to do so. A "master" is not always perfect by human standards, nor do they never err.

A person can be a master carpenter, yet not always smooth out every shaved corner. A master surgeon may be a life saver, yet sometimes make a bad cut, offer a misdiagnosis, or even make a fatal mistake. However, one should be pretty darn skilled in applying the art in life, and very much more skilled and competent than those without the skills required.

As in the martial arts, there is no technique in Zen to always avoid being hit or losing one's footing. Even less can we expect to win every battle. Rather, we are offered endless training on how to fall well.

Show me the man or woman who encounters life's obstacles—all the mess and mayhem of *samsara* (Buddhist lingo for this chaotic, often disappointing, ordinary world)—and is sometimes knocked sideways or down, but demonstrates how to recover well with the equanimity and insights that Zen wisdom offers, and I will show you a great Zen teacher (and Zen student, for the best Zen teachers never stop being students themselves).

That said, I believe that Dōgen's message is that although we are each the golden Buddha all the time, we should try to keep our corners smooth, make the right cut, avoid tripping and falling. A true master may miss, but rarely.

> [Though we speak of "being-time,"] do not mistakenly con-
> fuse it with "nonbeing," nor forcefully insist and label it as
> "being."

We provisionally speak of "being," but the Zen teachings ask us to step beyond and through all dichotomies, including being and not being, existence and non-existence. Such labels do not represent the whole of reality, and thus can limit us. There is something wondrous when we move past our narrow ideas of "to be or not to be." Hamlet would have had more options if he had been a Zen practitioner! In response to Shakespeare's existential query, a Zen master might yell or draw a circle in the air. Nonetheless, for practical purposes, we speak of being and passing time. In a famous kōan:

Master Shoushan held up his staff before the assembled monks, then declared, "If you say this is a staff, you oppose its reality. Yet if you say this is not a staff, then you negate the fact. So I ask you, what is this?" (*Gateless Gate*, Case 43)

Only in Zen can we be late for a dental appointment to fix a bad tooth, yet simultaneously know that there is no time, no dentist or patient, no bad tooth, and nothing to fix. There is no tooth, yet how much it hurts! At the beating heart of being and not being, there is this being-non-being-time.

As to time, we strive to understand how it is ever passing, but fail to understand it as that which never comes and never arrives.

We see only the passing nature of time, but do not understand the timeless. We do not understand "not coming or going."

Even though our intellectual understanding is time, time does not depend on our intellectual understanding. Foolish humans recognize that time leaves and comes, but none has truly penetrated such truth as being-time abiding in its place in each moment. How much less might we truly experience time having passed through the gate [of all dualisms, including ignorance and its negation]. Even if people recognize the time-being abiding in its place in each moment, who could give living expression to this state of recognition? And even among those who can give living expression to this state for a long time, how many are still groping around looking for their original face? If you think of being-time in the way of ordinary people, even wisdom and enlightenment become only appearances in time that come and go.

A subtle passage that begins with Dōgen pointing out that, whatever this being-time and its workings are, they do not depend on our intellectual understanding, let alone our categorization. In experiencing this being-time, it is helpful to step beyond both the ideas of the enduring or the finite, the ephemeral and the eternal, the unmoving or moving, to experience something truly free of time. In doing so, we also discover that such total freedom from time is fully embodied in all finite things, passing moments, and the ephemeral events of our lives.

Dōgen says that to fully realize being-time, we must step past all dichotomies including "ignorance vs. enlightenment" or "original face." Enlightenment is not an event that comes at a certain time and lingers in our minds forever. Real insight is that which is within, beyond and through all coming and going amid all life's coming and going. And that is true whether we are a great Zen master, a child, teenager, a middle-aged person starting to wonder about the passing years and the meaning of it all, or a grandmother bouncing her grandchild on her knee. Maybe a grandmother can sense that there is something sacred, something timeless, about that moment and interaction.

> In short, when the mind is freed from the traps and cages [of categories, divisions, judgments, and dichotomies], then being-time is realized and thoroughly actualized. Even the kings of heaven and their retainers would not be left separated from the being-time right now in which you are now exerting yourself. In fact, the being-time of all beings throughout the world, all beings of land and sea, is realized and actualized through your own exertion right now. The many kinds of beings who live in being-time in darkness and in light, in this realm or any others, are all the realization and actualization of your effort. We should learn in practice that, without the moment-by-moment continuance of our own efforts in the present, not a single phenom-

enon could ever be realized or actualized from one moment
to the next, and nothing would flow.

First, Dōgen directs us to drop from mind the walls and barriers
that make us see division, as well as the assumption that time cannot
be fully contained and expressed in each drop of a single moment. In
Dōgen's sea, the whole ocean is comfortably held and fully flows
within each single atom of seawater.

I don't know if most physicists would agree, but certainly many
poets can: we learn to find the whole universe endlessly held in every
atom, all of life in each blade of green grass, the totality of time in each
heartbeat.

In these words, Dōgen expresses a deep vision of interconnection
and interdependence. We might picture the cosmos as a single vibrant
city in which intertwining streets run in all directions. Or as a grand
ecosystem in which each plant and tree depends, directly or indirectly,
on every other plant and tree in a vast chain. Remove or destroy one
part of the balanced system and its absence impacts all the rest. We
might not realize that even dipping our toes into the ocean changes
the whole ocean. The world is moved by us as we help move the world.
The city gives life to us, and we help bring life to the city. Dōgen ex-
tends his vision of interconnection from the bottom of the deepest
sea, to the darkest cave, to the highest heavens above and whole other
worlds, and even to realms unseen which may exist. Somehow, you
would have direct or indirect impact on them, and they on you.

Dōgen's vision of being-time is a vision of the great mutual support
and sustenance of all things. The blooming of a flower brings life to
the soil, even as the soil nurtures the flower. Without the flower, the
soil is but lifeless dust, while a flower without soil has no place to grow
and no sustenance. Likewise, all the creatures of the garden, from
worms to birds to bees, sustain and are sustained by all the others
through their daily activities. Even predators and their prey are all
part of the grand cycles of life and death. The cancer that grew within
me was not welcome. It was competing with me for its own survival,

yet it too was part of the chain, perhaps making sure that I won't over-
stay my welcome in this world. Since I am just the ecosystem of this
garden too, I can't ultimately object. May I someday be put in the
ground to feed the daisies. All our being-times interlock.

Perhaps this is why Zen practitioners feel such deep connection to
the mountains, rivers, and their temple gardens?

> We should not just feel that the passage of time from one
> moment to the next is like the movement from east to west
> of the wind or a rainstorm. The whole universe is not
> unmoving, for all is moving and changing, and the uni-
> verse is flowing from one moment to the next. An example
> of such a moment-by-moment passing of time is the spring.
> The spring has countless aspects arrayed as what we call
> "the passage of time." We must learn profoundly that the
> momentary passing of time continues with nothing exter-
> nal to it, and so when spring flows there is nothing outside
> of spring.
>
> The moment by moment passing of spring, for example,
> always passes moment by moment through spring itself.
> Although perhaps flowing itself and the momentary pass-
> ing of time need not be in spring, nonetheless flowing is
> occurring throughout spring. Accordingly, because spring
> embodies the momentary passing of time, passing time is
> being realized and actualized in each present moment of
> springtime here and now. The flowing of time occurs by
> spring, thus the flowing is completed and brought to frui-
> tion in just this moment of spring.
>
> We should learn this well from all angles. In your experi-
> ence of passing time, if you imagine that circumstances are
> just individual events and things that are outside you and
> pass on from moment to moment heading east through
> hundreds and thousands of worlds for hundreds and thou-

sands or myriads of eons, then you have failed to truly learn in practice this Buddha Way.

Your lifetime, like the springtime, is the completion and coming to fruition of each moment of time. This is Dōgen's way of reminding us that this moment is just this moment, with no before or after. When the world is flowing as a moment of spring, there is just spring. Do not think of summer or winter as spring. He said the same in his "Genjō Kōan": "We do not say that winter becomes spring, nor do we say that spring becomes summer." Winter is just winter, summer wholly summer, and spring is totally spring.

How wonderful it is to live life with such awareness, not always feeling that the years are flying by and asking where they've gone, but knowing that this moment does not fly away and go. This season is just this season—all the world flowing as this season and day and minute, with no before or after.

In every moment of life, there is no before or after. Thus, when you bounce a baby on your knee, or taste the sweetness of a cherry, experience the experience without before or after. How can we fail to be fully present in a moment when there is no thought of any other?

Dōgen also reminds us that our lifetime, like the springtime, is "the completion and coming to fruition of each moment of time." The moments of time of our own lifetime is the embodiment of flowing time, bringing time and the moment to life. We are not merely passive witnesses to time, but instead, bring life to life in the only time possible: right now.

However, although there is now only this moment of spring, spring is also change. Although spring is only spring, it is not silent and stagnant, but is blossoming, changing, flowing, springing forth. It is flowers growing, birds and bees mating, and time moving into summer, fall, winter, and spring again. While knowing the moment that is only spring, with no before or after, also know and do not resist the passage of time at any time. You cannot bounce that baby forever, nor will the baby remain a baby. In the next moment of life, we may taste something more bitter than a cherry. That is all of time too.

This is the time of your life, as you are the life of time.

> Once, the great master Yaoshan Weiyan went to visit Zen master Mazu Daoyi at the suggestion of great master Shitou, with whom he had studied. Yaoshan asked, "I have digested all the teachings of the three vehicles of Buddhism and the twelve divisions of the scriptures, but what was the ancestral master Bodhidharma's intention in coming to China from India in the West?"

Yaoshan had great intellectual understanding of Zen history and the many multifaceted Buddhist doctrines, yet he asks this most basic question on the heart of the matter: Why did our great Ancestor, Bodhidharma, bother to bring these Zen teachings from India to China so long ago? What's that journey really all about?

> Thus questioned, Mazu responded, "Sometimes I make him raise an eyebrow or wink an eye, and sometimes I do not make him raise an eyebrow or wink an eye. Sometimes to make him raise an eyebrow or wink an eye is what's right, sometimes to make him raise an eyebrow or wink an eye is not right."
>
> Hearing this, Yaoshan experienced a great realization and said to Mazu, "When I was Shitou's student, I was like a mosquito trying to bite an iron bull."
>
> [Dōgen comments:] What Mazu says is not the same as other people's words. His "eyebrows" and "eyes" are the mountains and oceans, because the mountains and oceans are his "eyebrows" and "eyes." This "make him raise an eyebrow" is to see the mountains, and "make him wink" is to understand the seas. The "right" answer truly is his, and he is actualized by having him raise the eyebrows and wink.

But neither does "not right" mean not having him raise the eyebrows and wink, and to not have him raise the eyebrows and wink does not mean "not right." All are equally the being-time. The mountains are time, and the oceans are time. Without time, the mountains and oceans could never exist, so we should not deny that time is existing in the mountains and oceans right here and now. If time were annihilated, the mountains and oceans would be annihilated, but as time is not annihilated, thus are the mountains and oceans preserved. This being so, the morning star appears, the Buddha Tathāgata appears, the eye appears and raising up a flower appears. Each is time and, were there no time, it could not be thus.

Dōgen plays on a cherished kōan about a Zen master who inquires into the real meaning of Zen, which somehow eluded him in all his studies of texts and theory. He asks why Bodhidharma bothered to come to China; in other words, what is Zen all about? The traditional response about eyebrows and such can have a direct meaning: Bodhidharma did nothing special. Traveling to China was the most natural of things, like winking. If he had not done it, something else would have taken place. On the other hand, our own simple acts of winking and looking can also be known as the Buddha looking and winking, Bodhidharma looking and winking, the whole universe looking and winking. Not doing so is still the ancient master's eyes and eyebrows not doing so, the whole universe not doing so. It is not a matter of our having to be aware of such fact all the time. Our face is still shared with the ancient master although we do not feel so in a particular moment. Even then, it is still Bodhidharma's eyes and eyebrows as our eyes and eyebrows.

Dōgen plays his "Zen jazz" to take this one step further. His eyes and eyebrows are the mountains and seas (and the whole world and all within it). Winking the eye is an ocean winking, and raising an eyebrow is raising a mountain. There may be right and wrong times to do or not do an action, but ultimately there are no "wrong times," for each time is its own time, and even "not doing" is the right doing of "not doing," and "wrong doing" is the right doing of a "wrong doing." (Nonetheless, Dōgen would often remind us to do what's right and avoid doing wrong, for doing so helps clarify the heart and mind.[6])

Dōgen says that eye and eyebrow, mountains, and sea are all time. It is obvious that, without time, none of these could have evolved or come to be. Thus, he states, "Without time, the mountains and oceans could never exist." But equally, without the motion of their (and our) evolving, time would have been frozen and never flowed. Thus, time needs us and is us, as much as we need time and are time. Dōgen says, "So we should not deny that time is existing in the mountains and oceans right here and now." It is existing as you and me too, here and now.

And so it is for all moments in time, such as when the Buddha, sitting under the bodhi tree, saw the morning star and realized the truth. It is said that after many long years of striving and pushing himself to the extremes of body and mind, the Buddha finally eased his heart under that tree. Seeing the clear light of the morning star in the sky, he said: "I and all sentient beings on earth, together, are enlightened at once." All are enlightened at once, for all are one in this being-time.

Years later, when the Buddha held up a flower and winked, Mahākāśyapa saw and understood with a smile. In that famous story, the Buddha silently held up a single flower as the wordless expression of the truth, and his disciple Mahākāśyapa understood and also expressed this silently. This encounter is said to mark the beginning of our Zen lineage.

> Zen Master Guixing of the Shexian region is the heir of Shoushan and a Dharma descendant of Linji. On one occasion he preached to the assembly:
> Sometimes the mind arrives but words do not.
> Sometimes the words arrive but the mind does not.
> Sometimes the mind and words are both present.

Sometimes the mind and the words are both absent.

[Dōgen Comments:] The mind and the words are both being-time. Presence and absence, arriving and not arriving, are all being-time. The moment of presence is not yet over, but the moment of absence has come. [Or the moment of arriving has not yet appeared, but the moment of non-arriving is here]. This mind is the donkey, the words are the horse [from the famous kōan, "What is the meaning of Buddhadharma? When the donkey has not yet left, the horse arrives."] Horses have been made into words and donkeys have been made into mind. Presence is not a matter of having come, and absence is not a matter of not having come. Being-time is thus.

Dōgen's emphasis remains on each of the "sometimes" moments of being-time, whereby each and all interpenetrate, interfuse, and inter-embody. The image of the donkey not having departed while the horse arrives may point to the nature of time and the fact that moments pass yet also go nowhere. I like them also as symbols of ceaseless practice, since enlightenment constantly arrives though it's always here. Perhaps the horse represents the arrival of enlightenment, even though we may remain ignorant asses in so many ways.

Time and this moment are always here, so like that donkey, they never leave. Nonetheless, all the things of this ordinary world come and go like the horse, and so time passes and moments come and go. Both ways of seeing are true, so both can occupy the same stall of the barn.

There is some disagreement among translators regarding this section and Dōgen's reference to presence and absence, words and mind. As can be seen through all of Dōgen's writings, he was not a supporter of the idea that Zen truth must always be beyond words. A well-turned word, phrase, or teaching can resonate and embody truth. Thus, perhaps Dōgen saying that the mind is the donkey and words are the horse means that sometimes the mind understands but the words are inadequate to express that understanding. Sometimes it's the other way around—we say words without really understanding them. Sometimes both words and mind capture truth, and our words are well spoken. But truth is not dependent on either words or the feelings of our heart and mind's understanding. Then, words are not even needed, so they are absent.

Dōgen mixes it up more, showing that all of this can be true at once. As should be obvious by now, Dōgen's being-time is Buddha, never going or coming anywhere on Buddha donkey, yet fully embodying time as life's Buddha horses come and go. I am reminded of another saying we encountered in "One Bright Pearl." We are "just the robber riding the robber's horse to chase the robber." In English we say "horses for courses." Different things are suited for different purposes. All these different ways of experiencing time are just so, and this is true whether life has us riding atop our steed like a great aristocrat, or when we are just feeling like a horse's ass.

> Being-time is just so. Arrival blocks arrival, but is not blocked by non-arrival. Non-arrival is blocked by non-arrival, but is not blocked by arrival. The mind demarcates the mind and thus the mind is seen. Words demarcate words, and thus words are seen. Restriction restricts restriction, and thus restriction is seen. Because restriction restricts restriction, there is being-time. Restriction is made use of by objective phenomena, but restrictions that restrict objective phenomena have never occurred. I meet with a human being, and a human being meets a human being. I meet myself, and a manifestation meets a manifestation. These facts too, could not be so without time.
>
> Furthermore, mind is the time of realizing the truth right here [Genjō Kōan], and words are the time of going beyond barriers. Arrivals are the time of escaping forms,

while non-arrivals are just this and free of this. In this way
should you understand and be being-time.

Dōgen's word-jazz plays some wild phrases toward the end of "Uji."
Like the "words and mind" which both arrive, let me tell you how
Dōgen's words play in my heart: I take him to mean that each phenomenon and event delineates itself in its place and time, standing
unhindered from all other phenomena and events. Each marks itself
out as a moment of time, able to stand in contrast with all other things
and moments.

Nonetheless, this mind is all truth manifested right here, and words
go beyond all barriers. Arrivals escape all forms, while the non-arrivals
are here and not here at once. There is an aspect to reality that is beyond all arriving or departing. Thus, arrivals are just arrivals unhindered by departures (likewise for departures which stand on their
own, unhindered by arrivals), while there is a reality which sweeps in
all arriving and departing as a single whole, thus arrivals are also departures, departures are shared faces of arrivals too. Likewise, people,
things, and moments are not merely people, things, and moments.
This is the jazz sound that Dōgen plays.

I believe this is simply Dōgen's way of expressing how each phenomenon and event, you and me, is wholly what it is, which is just
what it is, yet is also barrier-free and includes the whole world.

Dōgen then concludes with these words:

The venerable Ancestors have thus spoken these words, but
is there nothing left to say? Mind and words arriving partway are being-time.

Mind and words not partway arriving are being-time. In
such a way, you should explore what is being-time. To have
him raise eyebrows and wink is half of being-time. To have
him raise the eyebrows and wink is mistaken being-time.
Not to have him raise the eyebrows and wink is half of

being-time. Not to have him raise the eyebrows and wink is a total mistake.

Thus, to practice thoroughly, coming and going, and to practice thoroughly, arriving and not-arriving, is the time-being of this moment.

Written on the first day of winter, 1240, at Kōshō Hōrin Monastery.

In closing, Dōgen seeks simultaneously to do away with *and* preserve all categories and measures that describe the interpenetration of being-time in a world of categories and measures. Even when something is partial or mistaken, there is no half or part of being-time, for even half or partway is always a full measure. Winking and raising the eyebrows are just actions by one human being that take place in one moment and then another, yet they are also more than this.

"Being-time" is not merely philosophy or Dōgen's abstract words. Rather, it describes actual experiences of fluid time that we can realize in our zazen and bring into life.

All that came before or may yet come is realized in the pivot point of our every step and turn, right here and now, which is being-time. The being-time dance brings you to life, and your every move brings the dance to life. Your whirling twirls all the other dancers, near and far: all being-time. They twirl you. They each have their own being-time, while you have your own being-times renewed each moment as a fresh moment of being-time. All is just the great, ongoing, timeless dance of being-time—a dance that goes on and on, both before and after our time.

Please know this the next time you look in the mirror and see the blemishes of passing time. Give a little wink.

# Life and Death, and the Whole Works

This final chapter is about our final chapter:
Death.
Frightening, unwelcome, unavoidable, heartbreaking, devastating, painful, and ugly. *Fini*, kaput. The End. Period.

We dread death because we humans have evolved to fear for our own survival, to anticipate and run from pain, to be awed by our non-existence, to know sorrow at the loss of those we love. And although I could not, would not want to be anything but a human being who feels what a human being feels, still, I agree that death can be quite sad and frightening. Sometimes downright *terrifying*!

However, with a bit of practice and insight, we can also see death as joyous—as a cause for celebration, like a birthday, or any other life transition. Perhaps we can even welcome it with peace and equanimity, seeing it as a natural part of life. As the borders and resistance between us and the rest of the world drop away, a wonderfully embracing wisdom arises that can only be described as

149

fear-without-fear, welcoming of the unwelcome, a broken heart
which can never be broken, filled simultaneously with grief and joy,
pain and equanimity, and shining with a light that includes all the
world's beauty and ugliness.

This is a tale about death seen in such ways. And it is also a story
about:

Life!

Life is joyous..We welcome and celebrate it, and hopefully don't fear
it. We can also experience it with peace and equanimity, and see it as a
natural part of being human. Nonetheless, it too has its frightening,
unwelcome, heartbreaking, painful, and ugly face, which includes
death as part of it. It is the Buddha's and Dōgen's teaching that, since
we find ourselves alive for this time, we should live as gently as we can,
in balance and moderation, with all the grace and skill we can muster.

Even so, it is also the Buddha's teaching—and just common sense—
that nobody alive escapes from eventual death. Likewise with
sickness—we all get sick at one point or another. Nobody who lives
long enough can avoid an eventual encounter with sickness and death,
and, if they make it that far, old age. It is a scary prospect for most of
us, and it was this prospect which first set Śākyamuni on the road in
search of liberation.

The story goes that the Buddha, when still living a sheltered life as
a prince, happened to see an old man, a sick man, and a corpse, and
these visions shocked him. He asked himself why we need to suffer so
in this life. Eventually, he came up with the solution to this suffering,
an insight that remains the bedrock of the Buddhist path. He saw
beyond mere coming and going, time, sickness, birth and death. But
he didn't find a cure for old age, sickness, and death in this human
body and lifetime. He himself eventually became old, got sick, and
died. Shortly before his death at eighty, he is quoted in the *Mahāparinibbāṇa Sutta* as saying this about his aging and frail body:

Now I am frail, Ānanda, old, aged, far gone in years. This is
my eightieth year, and my life is spent. Even as an old cart,

Ānanda, is held together with much difficulty, so the body
of the Tathāgata is kept going only with supports. It is,
Ānanda, only when the Tathāgata, disregarding external
objects, with the cessation of certain feelings, attains to and
abides in the signless concentration of mind, that his body
is more comfortable.[7]

I believe that the last sentence refers to a deep form of concentration that the Buddha used to escape the pain of his body. In those
days, before modern medicine and analgesic treatments, it must have
been very difficult to assuage physical pain. It is still hard today for so
many people who suffer from chronic pain. The Buddha was no exception. (I am very glad that, when I had my surgery, I had other options. Even so, it hurt like the devil for a while.)

But concentration is not the only way that the Buddha found to see
through, and be liberated from, old age, sickness, and death. His liberation took place in the midst of old age, sickness, and death. How?
He saw through the borders and frictions between the personal self
and the world, so his desires for youth, health, and existence evapo-
rated. This is what we ourselves realize during zazen. We no longer
feel such separation between birth and death, and so it is hard to be
afraid of them!

I do not want to mislead you, however, and suggest that all the ordinary tensions, fear, sadness, and loss we normally experience will
somehow vanish with practice. When my mother was dying of cancer,
it was very sad. It was hard to accept she was sick when she was at the
height of her illness, and it was hard when the day came to stop further treatments. So I cried many times. Zen practice is not about cold
stoicism, and it doesn't numb us from ordinary human emotions and
caring. I want to be able to cry, because to cry is to be human.

Because we have these human bodies and brains that are hardwired to feel these emotions, I do not think that we can ever completely cease to feel them during life. And as we saw, even the Buddha
sometimes found something to complain about. But he and the

ancient Zen masters found a way to be free of friction even when experiencing friction, to be fearful while also fully free of fear, devoid of disappointment even when feeling ordinary human disappointment.

Through the practice of the Buddha Way, we encounter an overriding peace and wholeness that transcends birth and death; a joy that holds both happiness and sadness. At the same time, there is birth and there is death, there are happy days and sad days. I hope a little of that light can shine through your moments of darkness and grief.

There is a story in the sutras that speaks about this. Kisa Gotami was the wife of a wealthy man, and they lived near the Buddha. After losing her only child a few months after his birth, Kisa Gotami was so overwrought that people thought she had gone insane. A friend saw her distress and told her to find the Buddha, implying that he had the medicine she needed. Kisa Gotami went to see the Buddha and asked him for the medicine that would restore her child to life. In response, the Buddha told her to go from house to house to find a mustard seed from a dwelling where nobody had died. Kisa Gotami was heartened and began her search across town, thinking she would find the medicine she needed. But although the people she met all wished to give her a mustard seed, every single household she visited had known at least one death, so they couldn't fulfill her request. She then realized why the Buddha had sent her on this search. "There is no house where death does not come," she realized.

I also recall a story of my first teacher in Japan, Azuma Ikuo Roshi, of Sōjiji Monastery, which took place about thirty years ago. I remember how shocked I was one day when I saw Azuma Roshi—the first Japanese Zen master I'd ever met—get teary-eyed soon after his wife died. I had just arrived in Japan, and thought Zen teachers were above and beyond life and death. I said to him directly, "Roshi, I am so sorry that your wife has passed recently. However, I thought 'life and death' are but a dream, and you sometimes teach that they are. If so, why are you crying?" He responded, "Life and death are but a dream. Sometimes a very sad dream."

Foolish me. Death is like a dream from the viewpoint of the absolute whole, but it is sometimes a very bitter dream as the fellow dreamers we love drift away from us. To feel grief at the death of someone we love, even great and prolonged grief, is natural to the human condition. Likewise, to feel some ordinary fear in the face of a cancer diagnosis or a hungry tiger, because this is just how we are wired to react. I see nothing wrong in grieving when it is time to grieve, feeling fear when there is something to fear. In fact, to feel further ashamed for feeling grief or fear is but another kind of suffering—duḥkha on top of duḥkha! Let yourself be sad or afraid sometimes, for that sadness and fear are in themselves nothing to fear.

There are, however, excessive and destructive degrees of depression and anxiety that we can experience. Sometimes we become so overwhelmed with haunting grief, panic, or fear that seeking professional assistance might be helpful. In some situations, even zazen is not enough to deal with some of these strong emotions, so we can then use other measures to work with them. In such cases in which sadness and fear become more than one can bear, please see your doctor and follow her guidance on treatments to help.

But for ordinary degrees of sadness and fear, allow yourself to feel them and don't resist. Most healthy humans feel intense grief at the loss of someone they love. They feel afraid when the subject of death presents itself. That's okay. Simultaneously, sit zazen as you can, and know birth and death as just the flowing waves on the surface of a great sea. Therein lies freedom.

Dōgen presented his teachings on life and death in two marvelous short sections of his *Shōbōgenzō*. One is called "Zenki," which might be translated as "The Whole Works" or "The Total Function." The other is "Shōji," which means "Life and Death" or "Birth and Death." They are short, but their wisdom is boundless. In both, Dōgen presents a kind of existential philosophy of living and dying—realistic yet optimistic—on how to live in the time of life, how to be sick in the time of sickness, how to age in the time of aging, and how to die in the time of dying. He presents various true visions of life and death that are all powerful prescriptions of Buddha's medicine for duḥkha.

First, let us look at "Zenki," the total function of this life-self-world which we are and live. My teacher, Nishijima Roshi, once wrote:

> The *Zen* [of Zenki] means "all" or "total" and *ki* means "functions," so Zenki means "all functions" or "the total function." From the Buddhist standpoint, we can say that this world is the realization of all functions. Master Dōgen explained this state of the world, quoting the words of Master Engo Kokugon [Yuanwu Keqin] that life is the realization of all functions and death is the realization of all functions."[8]

Were I to summarize in a nutshell, everything in the universe is totally functioning as that particular thing in the universe, life is totally functioning as life, death is totally functioning as death, you are totally functioning as you. You and all beings are just totally doing what we do. And all combined is just the total functioning of the universe. Of course, we don't always feel that the world is so, thus we feel that something lacks.

Here are Dōgen's words:

> The Buddhas' great way, when completely penetrated, is liberation and is realization. This "liberation" means that life liberates life and death liberates death. Thus, there is getting out of life and death and entering right into life and death, both of which are perfectly penetrating the great Way. There is shedding life and death and there is crossing life and death, both of which are the great Way perfectly penetrated. Realization is just life and life is just realization. At such a moment of realization, there is nothing but the total realization of life, and there is nothing but the total realization of death.

This passage presents life and death as events that we transcend through liberation, while we also dive into both. I might paraphrase this passage as follows: the Buddha's truth, when perfectly understood, is both to see through this world and to live that truth while in this world. When properly seen, life is thus liberated while being life, and death is liberated while being death. Therefore, there is seeing through and beyond ideas of life and death, and there is diving right into life and death, all of which together is the Buddha's truth.

In other words, we can see beyond the rising waves of life, and the vanishing waves of death, to the sea that rolls on and on. From this perspective, the coming and going of life and death are like a dream, for nothing truly comes and goes, and all is the waters of these waters rolling on. However, from another perspective, there is still life and death, and this life and death is your life; so live it, dive right in, swim as best you can. It may be a dream, but fully dream that dream.

To make real the Buddha's truth in life is this life, and this life is for making real the Buddha's truth in action. At such a moment, there is nothing that is not the total actualization of life, and there is nothing that is not the total actualization of death.

Buddhist realization means to not only see through the phenomena of this world to their dreamlike states in unbroken wholeness. It is also to realize that everything in this life is the whole universe, all of reality, the whole dance of reality. So when there is life, that is the whole of reality actualizing life in that spot, and when there is death, it is the whole of reality pouring into the actualizing of death in that spot.

Thus, Dōgen continues:

> This pivot point causes life to be and causes death to be.
> This very moment when the pivot point is realized is not
> necessarily large and not necessarily small, is not necessar-
> ily as vast as the world and is not necessarily limited, is not
> necessarily long-lasting, is not necessarily short and brief.

I might express it: A "pivot point" is the place and instant where an action happens. Thus, each pivot point of the activity of our lives in each moment causes this life to be what's happening, and then death to be what is happening at the time of death. The action might be large or small, with greater and lesser obvious effects on this world, yet everything impacts everything somehow. As well, the moment of each happening in the pivot moment is beyond measure, because each event is also the whole of timeless reality happening in that place and time.

The world is the stage on which the dance of life is realized, so that the dancer's activities make life manifest, and the dancing of a death scene likewise makes death happen. Now, it might appear that the phenomena of this world are big and small, limited in space and lasting for some amount of time. However, because the whole show of reality pours into each step of each dancer, both big and small movements are actually the whole boundless spectacle.

> Life at this present moment exists at this pivot point, and this pivot point exists as life in this present moment. Life is not a manifesting of the present; and life is not a becoming. Rather, life is the manifesting of the total functions, and death is the manifesting of the total functions.

Or: Life in the present is happening in this present pivot point, and the present pivot point is life coming to life. But life is also neither coming nor going. Life is not just the present and is not a realization or manifestation of something outside it. Rather, life is the coming to life of the whole works and death is the coming to death of the whole works. ("Total functions" means something like all things of the universe doing their thing, i.e., the whole works working.)

In other words, life is what happens in this moment, here and now. But when seen in another way, there is no coming or going in the dance that rolls on. If life is the whole dance—the great dance—then it is not just limited to one place and one time, but is also present in all places and times. Life is the whole thing everywhere doing its thing, and death is the whole thing everywhere undoing this thing too.

> Please know that among the innumerable dharmas [phenomena] that are present in the self, there is life and there is death. Let us quietly ponder whether this present life and the miscellaneous real dharmas that are coexisting with this life, are together in life or not together in life. There is not a single moment, nor any single dharma, that is not altogether in life. There is not a single thing nor any state of mind, that is not altogether life.

"Dharma" here is phenomena, the constituent elements and events of life. So put another way: Life and death are two phenomena among all the phenomena of your self. But are life and death and all other phenomena part of life, or not part of life? In fact, there is not one thing, not one moment or state of mind that is not altogether life itself.

It seems that life and death are just two of the many things that happen in this world. In Dōgen's vision, they are two phenomena, but they also flow into all other things, and all other things are facets of each of them and all other things too, and all things are the whole works!

Maybe we could sum this up by saying simply: Life is everything and is in the action of living. Death is everything and is in this action of dying. So, liberation does not only mean to see through life and death, but rather, to live life as everything and die death as everything. We can be free from the life and death of this world of coming and going called samsara, and also jump in wholeheartedly into the events of this world.

> Life can be compared to a time when a person is sailing a boat. On this boat, you are working the sail, you manage the rudder, you are handling the pole. At the same time,

the boat is carrying you, and there is no "you" to sail without the boat. By your sailing of the boat, this boat is made to be a boat. Please study and understand profoundly just this instant of the present. Understand this fully. At this very instant, everything is nothing other than the world of the boat. The sky, the water, and the shore have all become this time of the boat, which is very different from what this time would be if there were no boat. Thus, life is what you make of it, and you are what life is making of you. While you are sailing in the boat, your body and mind, self and environment, are all essential pivot points of the boat; and the entire earth and all of space are all essential pivot points of the boat. That is to say, life is the self, and the self is life.

Dōgen presents a vivid image of life bringing life to life. And just as all things—the sea and shore and sky and wind and sail and sailor— are one with the boat, and the boat is just these things, your sailing of life brings all of that to life. In other words, it is all a big trip, all the sea seaing, and you as the traveler make the trip by your traveling. If we were to substitute the word "life" for "boat" in the above, it would read something like this:

Life is a person living life. In that life, you do things like walk and talk and climb mountains and fall in love, and your actions are bringing those actions to life. At each moment, this life and world is carrying you and there is no "you" apart from this life and world. Furthermore, your living is causing life to be life. At this moment there is nothing other than this moment of life in this world in the present. The whole world is this life and life brings the world to life. Everything in the world is the present moment of this life, and is very different from a world in which there would be no life. Thus, life is what you make of it, and you are what life is making of you. While you are living this life, your body and mind and all circumstances are all essential action points of life, as each and all is the whole earth and universe. The self is life and life is the self.

So, your sailing, your dancing, brings this life to life. Sailing on the waters, sailing across the stage, sail well, sail with care. You are the life of the world.

Dōgen then quotes another famous master:

> Zen Master Yuanwu Keqin said: "Life is the manifesting of the total functions, death is the manifesting of the total functions." We should clarify and master these words. To master them means this: The truth that "life is the manifesting of the total functions" has no beginning and end, and fills the whole earth and the whole of space. Yet that fact neither hinders "life being the manifesting of the total functions" nor hinders "death being the manifesting of the total functions." The time that death is the manifesting of the total functions—and although it then fills the whole earth and the whole of space—not only does not hinder "death being the manifesting of the total functions" but also does not hinder "life being the manifesting of the total functions." Therefore, life does not obstruct death and death does not obstruct life. The entirety of earth and the entirety of space are both present in life and present in death.
>
> However, it is not that one bit of the whole earth and one bit of the whole of space totally function in life on the one hand and totally function in death on the other hand. It is not one, but neither is there difference; there is not difference, but neither is it identical; it is not identical, but neither is it many. Thus, in life all dharmas [phenomena] are manifesting as the total functions, and in death all dharmas are manifesting as the total functions. As well, in the state beyond "life" and beyond "death" there is the

manifesting of the total functions. In the manifesting of
the total functions, there is life and there is death.

In other words: Life is the whole works, and death is the whole
works, and they don't get in each other's way. The whole works is also
the whole works and does not get in its way.

This reminds me of Dōgen's description of the time of birth and
death in his "Genjō Kōan":

> Thus, it is an established rule in Buddhist teachings to deny
> that birth turns into death. Therefore, birth is understood
> as no-birth, for in the time of birth there is no other
> moment with which to compare it. It is an unshakable
> teaching in Buddha's preaching that death does not turn
> into birth. Therefore, death is understood as no-death
> when there is no other moment with which to compare it.
> Birth is a situation complete in this moment. Death is a sit-
> uation complete in this moment. They are the same as win-
> ter and spring. We do not say that winter becomes spring,
> nor do we say that spring becomes summer.

Each moment of birth and death is complete in its respective moment, and its respective whole moment is complete in that moment.
Nonetheless, they do not obstruct each other's moment. Likewise,
they are each other, and are all things.

Dōgen concludes:

> For this reason, the total functions of life and death are like
> a vigorous youth bending and extending an arm. Or "like a
> person at night reaching back to search for a pillow."

These expressions imply that life and death just function as the
most natural of things, each just doing its thing as the ordinary (yet
amazing!) manifesting of all things doing.

They manifest themselves with immeasurable, abundant mystical power and wondrous light.

Dōgen frequently points out that the most magical of mystical powers is not to levitate, walk on water, or foresee the future— assuming we could do any of these—but simply to perform countless ordinary and natural actions which, when we reflect on it, are truly amazing. How much of a miracle is it that we are here, able to breathe, laugh, cry, and drink a cup of tea? It has taken all the physics and chemistry, time, and circumstances of the universe to allow us to be here, doing a simple act like drinking a cup of tea. All the heat and light, twists and turns of the universe also work to bring us to the mysterious miracle of death. So, all of life and death are our "mystical powers." This is especially true when we use these ordinary powers for good, such as to bring a bit more strength, kindness, and compassion into the world.

> In the very moment of manifesting, because total functions are being manifested as this manifesting itself, we may feel that there was no manifestation before this manifestation. However, the state before this manifestation was just the previous manifesting of total functions. Although there has been previous manifesting of the total functions, they do not obstruct the present manifesting of total functions. Thus, such views and understandings just manifest moment following moment.

I take this to mean that when we experience a moment of realization of the whole works working in that particular moment, it feels like there is no before or after. However, felt or unfelt, this same realization applies to the next moment, and the moments before or after this moment as well. All are the whole works working, and they do not get in the way of this present moment here and now of the whole works working.

The above was written by Dōgen in 1243.

I hope that the basic point of "The Whole Works" shines through: Your birth and everything that has happened to you in life, your health and sickness, your youth or old age, your being rich or poor, as well as everything that will happen in the future—all of it is the whole world, the whole universe, the whole dance dancing, the whole of reality fully doing its thing in that moment. In that moment there is nothing else but complete moments of whole functioning. Let us try to see beyond each separate thing and event so that there is no separation, no coming and going, no birth and death, but also see it all as everything and each other thing.

Dōgen continued this theme in another writing called "Shōji" (Life and Death), which begins:

> Because Buddha is in birth and death, thus there is no birth and death. It is also said that, because there is no "Buddha" in birth and death, thus there is no delusion in birth and death. These are the words of Jiashan Shanhui and Dingshan Shenying, two great Zen masters. Do not fail to pay heed to these words as those of people who have attained the way. If you wish to be free from birth and death, then these words must become clear to you.

In Buddha, the great sea flowing, the whole dance dancing beyond this and that, coming and going, there is no birth and death. The ocean is not born and does not die, although waves appear to rise and fall upon its surface. The dance dances on beyond any one of its dancers. However, Dōgen was never one for stopping at just such a one-sided realization. Rather, he said we must come back to life, put aside visions of Buddha and sea as anything other than life and death themselves, and realize life as life living and death as death deathing too. All is the sea seaing, the dance dancing.

These words echo the famous opening lines of Master Dōgen's "Genjō Kōan":

When things are seen as separate in the Buddha's teachings
... there is birth and there is death, and there are Buddhas
and sentient beings. When the myriad things are realized
as each without an individual self, there is . . . no Buddhas
and no sentient beings, no birth and no death. In the Buddha Way, we must leap clear of and right through both the
view of fullness and the view of lack; thus there are again
birth and death . . . sentient beings and Buddhas. Yet even
so, the beloved flowers still fall to our regret and sorrow, the
weeds still grow though we wish it were not so.

In Dōgen's way, we do not seek to escape life nor flee from death,
but dive right in, finding all of reality there. I take this passage to
mean that we radically jump beyond any idea of life, death, and Buddha as separate things—that there is no mere idea of Buddha that is in
any way apart from life and death. Life and death then become the
whole works, and we truly understand their sacred nature. We don't
even run from the natural regret and sorrow we encounter as life's
beloved flowers fall.

He continues:

If a person searches for Buddha somewhere outside of birth
and death, that is like pointing your cart north when wishing to head to a southern country, or like looking south
when wanting to see the North Star. It is just amassing ever
more causes of birth and death, and to have completely lost
the path of liberation.

Many of us seek to get free from suffering in this world by trying to
get to some state or realm where all our suffering completely vanishes,
fully and forever. In fact, there is such a realm and state, but we continue to live our life in this world where flowers fall and sad things
happen too. Suffering completely vanished, fully and forever, and our
continued life in this world of ongoing suffering, prove to be the same

place beheld by a Buddha or by ordinary people. We can even experience this world both ways at once, beyond one way or two ways, seeing with the eyes of both Buddha and ordinary people at once. In fact, both aspects are the same single reality, like two sides which constitute the same one coin all along. The Buddha ocean truly is present always, still and silent, although we sometimes become swept up in the storming waves that appear on its surface. Often, in the storm and sadness, we can lose sight of the silence and peace that are also always present. We may seek hard for the silence and peace, believing falsely that the only way to find such is to run totally away from the storms and troubles of this world. However, Dōgen advises us to forget about some other state or realm as something far away, and to see and experience Buddha right here in all of life's separation and division, coming and going. Birth and death, in and of themselves, are this truth too. This is a profound nondualism. To miss that fact is simply to go the wrong way, look in the wrong places. By dividing things, separating life and death from some other state or realm, we actually increase the feelings of separation and division, and all the accompanying friction and alienation. Doing so causes us to feel lost in a world in which life is clung to and death is feared. To know true unity free of friction and alienation, find the whole works in each separate thing, including life and death right here.

> Just understand that only life and death themselves are nirvana, there is nothing to be avoided as life and death, and nothing to seek and aspire to as nirvana. Then, for the first time upon realizing this, you are free from life and death.

Dōgen could not lay it out any more directly. If I were to get a tattoo, I think I'd have it say, "Life and death are nirvana."

Next, Dōgen returns to his view of every event that happens being all of time in that moment. We have encountered this teaching many times in his writings. He presents a worldview in which every event, as it is happening, is its own complete world of time.

It is a mistake to think that we move from birth to death. Birth is a state of one time with its own past and future. For this reason, in the Buddha's teachings, it is said that life is not life, birth itself is unborn. Death is also a state of one time with its own past and future. That is why it is said that death is not death.

If each happening is the whole works in one time fully contained therein, then each happening happens, yet does not happen. It is like saying that "this" wave heading from here to there is the whole sea flowing, and "that" wave heading from there to here is the whole sea flowing, so each wave's rising and falling is really not rising and falling, for there is just the whole sea flowing. At the same time, "this" wave is the whole sea flowing then and there, with its own past and future, so there is nothing else. It is the same for all the events of life.

Note that the translation of Shōji switches in a few places from "life" to "birth." In fact, the Chinese character for the sho (生) of Shōji (生死) is ambiguous in that it can mean both "life" in general, but also "birth" into life. So, the above can also read, "Life is a state of one time with its own past and future. For this reason, in the Buddha's teachings, it is said that life itself is not life."

Thus, in the time that is called life, there is only life. In the time called death, there is only death. Thus, when life comes there is just life, and when death comes just actualize death. Thereby, do not fight them, do not serve them, neither need you wish for them.

Since life in the time of life is the whole works and death in the time of death is the whole works, in the time of life there is nothing but life, and in the time of death there is nothing but death. Since the dancer rising is the whole dance rising, and the dancer descending is the whole dance's descending, in the time of rising there is just wholly rising, and in the time of descending there is thoroughly descending.

This leads to a wonderful experience of transcendence where we neither fight nor resist the experience of either life or death; we do not become their prisoner; nor do we wish for and run toward one or the other. That last line is so fantastic, I might add it to my tattoo: "Do not fight them, do not serve them, neither need you wish for them."

> This life and death is itself the life of Buddha. If we despise such and want to run from such, that is just wanting to flee the life of Buddha. If we cling to one, if we try to remain in one, this is also losing the life of Buddha. We confine ourselves to the mere surface of Buddha. But when we are without aversion and without longing, then we enter the mind of Buddha for the first time.

Life is the life of Buddha and death is the life of Buddha. Do not despise and want to run from death (or run from life either). Do not cling to life and want to remain there (same for death). When seeing each and all as just the life of Buddha, neither running toward nor running away from, but diving right in, such is the mind of Buddha.

> But do not measure it with thoughts, getting lost in intellectual understanding, and do not try to express it with words! When we just let go of our bodies and our minds and cast them into the abode of Buddha, then everything is done by Buddha. Thereupon, when one follows and flows with this, not struggling in effort or mind, we are free from life and death and become Buddha. Who could then experience obstacles cluttering the mind?

Put aside mere intellectual understanding and don't just turn this into a saying. A slogan on a tattoo alone won't cut it, for it is how we walk the walk that proves this whole wild trip. Thinking about dancing is not dancing. We should dedicate our whole body and mind to the dance. So drop all aversions and attractions—thus dropping bodymind—and realize that the whole works is running the whole works. Then, just flow with the flowing where the dancing flows, dance Buddha where Buddha dances, dance through life and death.

> There is a very simple way to become Buddha. Do not commit unwholesome actions; be without attachment to life and death; show profound compassion for all sentient beings; respect those above and have pity for those below; do not have a heart of likes and dislikes, aversions or desires, nor thoughts and worries about things. This is to become Buddha. Do not search someplace else.

In Dōgen's vision of enlightenment, it is not enough simply to realize that we are all originally Buddha and have been all along. It is vital that we act accordingly and bring Buddha to life in this life through our good and gentle thoughts, words and actions. So here he prescribes his "simple way" for doing so. First, be gentle, and avoid the wrongs committed through excess desire, anger, jealousy, and other examples of divided thinking. Next, do not be attached to life and death, or any things or events contained therein. That does not mean that we should become dispassionate and detached from life. We can still love and savor the events of this life and enjoy the people we love. However, we should also learn equanimity and flow with whatever life brings.

Dōgen advises that we respect those who deserve respect and take pity on those in need. But, at the same time, we should be free of aversion and excess attractions, seeing past hopes and fears, worries and grief. When we do so, there is nothing more to seek.

So said Dōgen in this undated text.

Thus, let us see each moment of life and death as sacred, with the whole of the universe pouring into each drop. Learn to allow it all to flow. When we experience this life in such a way, there is freedom.

Finally, let us end at the end, which may be a new beginning:

I am often asked about rebirth, and the Buddhist vision of possible future lives after this one. Do I believe in such things?

From his writings, it seems that Master Dōgen certainly held some deep belief that human beings are reborn, and that before this life we had a series of past lives. Our good and bad actions in this and previous lives lead to good and bad effects in this and future lives. That belief is very clear in some of his writings, and it is not surprising coming from a man of his day and times. In fact, perhaps the majority of Buddhists today still have such beliefs and consider them vital to being a Buddhist, especially in places like Thailand and Tibet.

However, the idea of rebirth did not seem to be so important to Dōgen or most of the other ancient Zen masters, and it is not really very important to me. Why?

All these many masters were focused on the possibility of liberation in this life, here and now, and action in the present world, whether or not there are future lives and worlds to come. If there is a time to manifest good and avoid evil, it is in this life. Whether there are future lives or no future lives, we can leap beyond that fact by focusing on what happens now. Whether our lives are the product of past karma or not, we can free ourselves and change our paths by how we think, speak, and act now and into the future. Liberation is available now. This is the pivot point, here and now.

I am skeptical of many of the more literal or detailed Buddhist claims that describe the mechanism of rebirth (although my mind is open to any possibility). However, I do know that this life is not only as it appears—I hope that fact is clear from what you have encountered in this book—and that there is more to who we are than meets the eye.

Master Dōgen repeatedly points out to us that this life is like a dream, as is birth and death, yet they are a real dream. The things that happen in the dream have real effects upon us dreamers. Thus, I believe that our actions have effects, and I believe that we create "heavens" and "hells." I see people create "hells" within themselves all the time, and hellish situations for their family and others around them, by their acts of greed, anger, and ignorance. I see people who live in this world as "hungry ghosts," never satisfied. Traditionally, Buddhists said that, due to our greedy acts, we may be reborn after death as "hungry ghosts" who can never be satiated. Our runaway instincts and ferocity might result in rebirth as a wild animal in some next life. Our good behavior may lead to various pleasant heavens. Well, putting aside any future lives, I see people who behave like animals or insatiable ghosts or angels in this one.

I also believe, as did Dōgen, that we are reborn moment by moment, so in that way, we are constantly reborn, always changing. The "Jundo" who began writing this book, or this sentence, is not the same "Jundo" who finished them. Furthermore, I believe that my actions will continue to have effects on this world long after this body is in its grave.

I also believe that as we are all the great dance, we are all each and everything that is happening, has happened, or will happen. This is Master Dōgen's other great vision that, I hope, has come pouring forth from every page of his words in this book. Every blade of grass, every grain of dust on a distant planet, every child born today, long ago, or who will be born in the far future, every ancient mountain or future machine, is us and is life. They are, each and all, as much you as every hair on your head is you, every cell within you is you, the child who was you is you, the dust and ashes that will be you are you, every heartbeat is you. You may not feel it is so, just as you are not aware of each of the trillions and trillions of cells that make you into you, but they are certainly you. And, though it is equally hard to see and feel sometimes, you and I do not just begin and end at the surface of the skin, at the moment of birth or with our final breaths.

But what about those posited future lives, heavens and hells? Will I be reborn as a god, a hungry ghost, a fish or wild fox, or another human being? My attitude, and that of many other Buddhist teachers these days, is that whether or not there are future lives, heavens and hells, live this life here and now, seek not to do harm, seek not to build "heavens" and "hells" in this world, and let what happens after death take care of itself. If there are no future lives, no heavens or hells, live this life here and now, seek not to do harm, seek not to build "heavens" and "hells" in this world, let what happens after death take care of itself.

Thus I do not much care whether avoiding harm and being gentle will buy me a ticket to heaven and keep me out of hell, but I know for a fact that they will go far in this life. And if there is a "heaven and hell" in the next life, or other effects of karma now or later, well, my actions now have effects there too, and might be the ticket to heaven or a good rebirth should that prove so.

It remains a mystery today, now as much as in the Buddha or Dōgen's day, why some people are born to good circumstances, while others are not. Bad things sometimes happen to good people, and some who do evil seem to thrive. "God's mysterious plan" or the "karma of past lives" have both been offered by many thinkers and sages to explain why. It could be that these are true. Or, it might just be the luck of the draw, just as some seeds scattered by nature on the ground grow big and strong, while others never sprout, give rise to the small and weak, or serve as meals for the birds. Personally, I tend to feel that the human condition is made up of seeds of life scattered by the universe, and our fate and the fates of the carrots and peas are not so different.

Some scholars believe that, rather than being a literal description of a mechanism for postmortem rebirth, the Buddhist teachings on rebirth were simply meant as ethical statements encouraging good behavior, or as consolation to make us feel better about the reasons for our lives' ups and downs—the wealth and health which seem to come or go out of the blue. I tend to feel the same way.

However, I also believe that we are literally born as all things. Every seed gives life to the whole garden, the whole universe. Further, our wisdom and good actions now do have good effects on ourselves and the world, and determine how we live and experience this life. Now is the pivot point of all times. I feel that Master Dōgen felt much the same. In other words, whatever the truth, live in a gentle way, avoiding harm to self and others, seeking to avoid harm now and in the future too. See through this world of birth and death, good and bad, to the light which shines in all things, all while trying to make this world and life a bit better.

That, I believe, was Dōgen's core message:
Dance with grace right now.

And so, to dance . . .

Everything has been said.
Time to sit now.
Time to dance.

# Acknowledgments

I would like to thank my wife, Mina Yamaguchi, my children, Leon and Sada, Gudo Wafu Nishijima Roshi, Doshin Cantor Roshi, Ikuo Azuma Roshi, Jiho Sargent Roshi, Daiho Hilbert Roshi, my friends along the way at Treeleaf Sangha, including our priests who keep the flame burning and our many sitters who support each other. I especially would like to thank Kirk McElhearn, a long-time Zen practitioner and editor, for bringing all the care and diligence of Dōgen's way to the first version of this manuscript, copyeditor Vanessa Zuisei Goddard, Josh Bartok, and all the folks at Wisdom Publications. I also thank the farmers and clerks, doctors and nurses, scientists and truck drivers, artists and artisans, flowers and weeds, both the moments we love and the moments which scare us, ants and fish, stones, rivers, stars, cells and celestial planets, all persons and things named or unnamed, whether in time and timeless, for we are all interdependent and interidentical as this Great Dance.

# Notes

1. Quoted here: https://tricycle.org/magazine/you.
2. *Dōgen's Extensive Record*, trans. Leighton and Okumura, 308.
3. Hee-jin Kim, "The Reason of Words and Letters: Dōgen and Kōan Language," in *Dōgen Studies*, ed. William R. LaFleur (Honolulu: University of Hawaii, 1985), 60.
4. Based on Taigen Leighton's *Cultivating the Empty Field*, 72–73.
5. For example, in *Shōbōgenzō* "Sansui kyō" (The Mountains and Waters Sutra).
6. cf. Master Dōgen's *Shōbōgenzō* "Shoaku makusa."
7. From the Maha-parinibbana Sutta (Last Days of the Buddha), trans. Sister Vajira and Francis Story (Kandy: Buddhist Publication Society, 1998).
8. From the Nishijima-Cross translation of Master Dōgen's *Shōbōgenzō*, vol. 2, 285.

# Sources

I would like to thank the authors and editors of the following books and translations which were so helpful to consult in the writing of this book:

Bielefeldt, Carl. *Dōgen's Manuals of Zen Meditation*. Oakland: University of California Press, 1988.
———, trans. "Shōbōgenzō zanmai ō zanmai: King of Samādhis Samādhi." *Dharma Eye* 18 (Autumn, 2006).
Cook, Francis H. *Sounds of Valley Streams*. New York: State University of New York Press, 1989.
———. *How to Raise an Ox: Zen Practice as Taught in Zen Master Dōgen's Shōbōgenzō*. Somerville, MA: Wisdom Publications, 2002.
Hoshin, Anzan, and Joshu Dainen Yasuda. "Tenzo Kyōkun: Instructions for the Tenzo." https://wwzc.org/dharma-text/tenzo-kyōkun-instructions-tenzo. In *Cooking Zen*. Ottawa: Great Matter Publications, 1996.
———. "Shoji: Birth and Death." https://wwzc.org/dharma-text/shoji-birth-and-death-生死.
Leighton, Taigen Dan. *Cultivating the Empty Field: The Silent Illumination of Zen Master Hongzhi*. Boston: Tuttle Publications, 2000.
———. *Visions of Awakening Space and Time: Dōgen and the Lotus Sutra*. New York: Oxford University Press, 2007.
Leighton, Taigen Dan, and Shōhaku Okumura. *Dōgen's Pure Standards for the Zen Community: A Translation of Eihei Shingi*. Albany: State University of New York Press, 1996.
———. *Dōgen's Extensive Record: A Translation of the Eihei Kōroku*. Somerville: Wisdom Publications, 2010.
Masunaga, Reiho. *Shōbōgenzō: The Sōtō Approach to Zen*. Tokyo: Layman Buddhist Society Press, 1958.

Nearman, Hubert. *Shōbōgenzō: The Treasure House of the Eye of the True Teaching.* Mount Shasta, CA: Shasta Abbey Press, 2007.

Nishijima, Gudo, and Chodo Cross. *Master Dōgen's Shōbōgenzō*, 4 vols. San Francisco: Windbell, 1994–1999. These volumes are also available online through the Bukkyō Dendō Kyōkai (Society for the Promotion of Buddhism) at https://www.bdkamerica.org/book-product?title=&field_book_taisho_tid=217&taxonomy_catalog_tid=247.

Nishiyama, Kosen, and John Stevens. *Shōbōgenzō: The Eye and Treasury of the True Law*, 4 vols. Japan: Nakayama Shobo. 1975–1983.

Okumura, Shōhaku. *Realizing Genjōkōan: The Key to Dōgen's Shōbōgenzō.* Somerville: Wisdom Publications, 2010.

——. *The Mountains and Waters Sutra: A Practitioner's Guide to Dōgen's "Sansuikyō."* Somerville: Wisdom Publications, 2018.

Tanahashi, Kazuaki. *Moon in a Dewdrop: Writings of Zen Master Dōgen.* New York: North Point Press, 1985.

——. *Enlightenment Unfolds: The Essential Teachings of Zen Master Dōgen.* Denver, CO: Shambhala Publications, 2000.

——. *Beyond Thinking: A Guide to Zen Meditation by Zen Master Dōgen.* Denver: Shambhala Publications, 2004.

Tanahashi, Kazuaki, and the San Francisco Zen Center. *Treasury of the True Dharma Eye: Zen Master Dōgen's Shobo Genzo*, 2 vols. Denver: Shambhala Publications, 2013.

Yokoi, Yūhō. *The Shobo-genzo*, 5 vols. Japan: Sankibo Press, 1986.

Finally, many of the translations of the Sōtō Zen Text Project were useful in their online draft versions, which are no longer available. These translations will appear in the project's forthcoming publications of the *Denkō roku* and *Shōbōgenzō.*

# Index

on acceptance, 104–5
birth and death and, 160, 162–63
Buddha and, 160, 162–63
core message, 52
dance and, 70, 102
enlightenment and, 16, 51, 104
medicine in, 71–72
opening lines, 162–63
overview, 16
*shikantaza* and, 71
goallessness, 23, 24, 28, 29, 37, 38, 47, 82
goals, 4, 56, 57
chasing, 4
Guixing of Shexian, 144–45

**H**
*Hamlet* (Shakespeare), 97
heavens, 30–31
and hells, 168–70
Hendrix, Jimi, 7
"Hokke-Ten-Hokke" (Dōgen), 10–11
Huayan Buddhism, 15, 73, 78
"hungry ghosts," 169

**I**
illness. *See* cancer; dis-ease
Indra, 8
Indra's Net of jewels, 73, 74
interflowing, 16, 118, 120, 125

**J**
jazz, 6, 71. *See also* "word-jazz"; "Zen jazz"
Joyce, James, 7

**K**
kalpas, 87, 106
karma, 129–30, 170
karmic consciousness, deluded, 107, 108
Kesa Gomati/Kisa Gotami, 152
Kim, Hee-jin, 75
kōans, 42, 91–92, 106, 108, 136–37, 143, 145

Dōgen and, 7, 44, 86 (*see also* "Genjō Kōan")
sitting as a realized kōan, 44
understanding the meaning of, 45
zazen and, 44, 45
Koshu Yō, 51

**L**
letting thoughts go, 23, 26–28
liberation, 168
bodhisattvas and, 100
Buddha's, 150, 151, 154
Buddha's truth and, 155
life, birth, death, and, 154–55, 157, 163
*See also under* suffering
life
compared with dreams, 152, 155, 168
compared with the sea, 64, 127, 158, 165
dance and, 14, 19, 66, 156, 159
resistance to, 36, 166
*See also* birth, life, and death
life-self-world, 59, 154
Longji, 106
lotus flower, 58
lotus posture, 23, 38, 39, 44, 75, 76, 78, 84
*Lotus Sutra*, 10, 12, 13, 112, 113

**M**
*Mahāparinibbāṇa Sutta*, 150–51
Mahayana Buddhism, 100
"Buddha" and, 30
Dōgen and, 5–7, 9, 12, 13, 75
Seven Buddhas in, 86
wisdom and, 9, 13
Manjuśrī, 44–45
Māra (demon), 84
meditation, 81
Buddha's, 22, 87
goals of, 81, 87
*shikantaza* and, 23, 26, 28, 37, 43, 81, 87
sitting and, 25, 87, 88

# About the Author

Jundo Cohen is a Zen teacher and founder of the Treeleaf Zendo, a Sōtō Zen community using visual media to link Zen practitioners around the world. Treeleaf serves those who cannot easily commute to a Zen center due to health concerns; age or disability; living in remote areas; or work, childcare, or family needs; and provides zazen sittings, retreats, discussion, interaction with a teacher, and all other activities of a Zen Buddhist sangha, all fully online without thought of location or distance. Jundo was born and raised in the United States but has lived in Japan for more than half his life. He was ordained and subsequently received Dharma transmission from Master Gudo Wafu Nishijima and is a member of the Sōtō Zen Buddhist Association.

# What to Read Next
# from Wisdom Publications

**Hardcore Zen**
*Punk Rock, Monster Movies, and the Truth About Reality*
Brad Warner

"*Hardcore Zen* is to Buddhism what the Ramones were to rock and roll: A clear-cut, no-bulls**t offering of truth." —Miguel Chen, Teenage Bottlerocket

**Realizing Genjokoan**
*The Key to Dōgen's Shōbōgenzō*
Shohaku Okumura

"A stunning commentary. Like all masterful commentaries, this one finds in the few short lines of the text the entire span of the Buddhist teachings." —*Buddhadharma: The Practitioner's Quarterly*

**Being-Time**
*A Practitioner's Guide to Dogen's Shobogenzo Uji*
Shinshu Roberts

"This book is a great achievement. Articulate, nuanced, and wonderful." —Jan Chozen Bays, author of *Mindfulness on the Go*

**Opening the Hand of Thought**
*Foundations of Zen Buddhist Practice*
Kosho Uchiyama
Translated and edited by Tom Wright, Jisho Warner, and Shohaku Okumura

"If you read one book on Zen this year, this should be that book."
—James Ishmael Ford, head teacher, Boundless Way Zen, and author of *If You're Lucky, Your Heart Will Break*


**The Grand Delusion**
*What We Know But Don't Believe*
Steve Hagen

*The Grand Delusion* helps readers cut through age-old and seemingly intractable questions from science, philosophy, and religions—about life, the universe, and everything.


**Deepest Practice, Deepest Wisdom**
*Three Fascicles from Shobogenzo with Commentary*
Kosho Uchiyama
Translated by Shohaku Okumura and Tom Wright

"*Real Dharma.* The mingled voices of these teachers—inspiring, challenging, sage, and earthy—shake dust from the mind so we may see more clearly what's right here." —Ben Connelly, author of *Inside Vasubandhu's Yogacara: A Practitioner's Guide*

# About Wisdom Publications

Wisdom Publications is the leading publisher of classic and contemporary Buddhist books and practical works on mindfulness. To learn more about us or to explore our other books, please visit our website at wisdomexperience.org or contact us at the address below.

Wisdom Publications
199 Elm Street
Somerville, MA 02144 USA

We are a 501(c)(3) organization, and donations in support of our mission are tax deductible.

Wisdom Publications is affiliated with the Foundation for the Preservation of the Mahayana Tradition (FPMT).